great performances

Creating Classroom-Based Assessment Tasks

Larry Lewin • Betty Jean Shoemaker

 Association for Supervision and Curriculum Development • Alexandria, Virginia USA

Association for Supervision and Curriculum Development
1703 N. Beauregard St. • Alexandria, VA 22311-1714 USA
Telephone: 1-800-933-2723 or 703-578-9600 • Fax: 703-575-5400
Web site: http://www.ascd.org • E-mail: member@ascd.org

Gene R. Carter, *Executive Director*
Michelle Terry, *Associate Executive Director, Program Development*
Nancy Modrak, *Director, Publishing*
John O'Neil, *Director of Acquisitions*
Julie Houtz, *Managing Editor of Books*
Jo Ann Irick Jones, *Senior Associate Editor*
Charles D. Halverson, *Project Assistant*
Gary Bloom, *Director, Design and Production Services*
Karen Monaco, *Senior Designer*
Tracey A. Smith, *Production Manager*
Dina Murray, *Production Coordinator*
John Franklin, *Production Coordinator*
Valerie Sprague, *Desktop Publisher*
Nedalina Dineva, M. L. Coughlin Editorial Services, *Indexer*

Printed in the United States of America.

December 1998 member book (p). ASCD Premium, Comprehensive, and Regular members periodically receive ASCD books as part of their membership benefits. No. FY99-3.

ASCD Stock No. 198184
ASCD member price: $14.95   nonmember price: $17.95

Library of Congress Cataloging-in-Publication Data
Lewin, Larry.
      Great performances : creating classroom-based assessment tasks
/ Larry Lewin, Betty Jean Shoemaker.
      p. cm.
      Includes bibliographical references.

      ISBN 0-87120-339-1
      1. Educational tests and measurements—United States. 2. Grading
and marketing (Students)—United States. I. Shoemaker, Betty Jean.
II. Title.
      LB3051 .L462 1998
      371.3—ddc21

                                                      98-40133
                                                        CIP

02 01 00 99 98   5 4 3 2 1

Great Performances: Creating Classroom-Based Assessment Tasks

Larry Lewin
Betty Jean Shoemaker

Acknowledgments

We would like to gratefully acknowledge our elementary, middle, and high school students, who have contributed significantly to our growth as teachers. We also acknowledge the contribution of many excellent teachers, too numerous to list, who have shared their curriculum and assessment ideas freely with us.

We would also like to acknowledge the love, understanding, and support provided by our families, in particular Linda Barber, and Timothy and Theresa Shoemaker, as we completed this manuscript.

Thank you to Jo Ann Mazzarella, our colleague in Eugene School District 4J, for text editing our rough draft; to John O'Neil, ASCD director of acquisitions, who initiated and launched this book with his advice and good counsel; to Jo Ann Jones, ASCD senior associate editor, who steered this book from rough draft to final copy with dedication and care; and to Nancy Modrak, ASCD's director of publishing.

—Larry Lewin and Betty Jean Shoemaker

Thanks to my many colleagues and teacher friends, especially the teachers and staff at Monroe Middle School in Eugene, Oregon; to Teresa Smith, my principal who supported and encouraged me; to Tanis Knight, my first teaching partner, coauthor, and inspiration; to her husband Dick Sagor, advice sharer and witty observer; to Vicky Ayers, who taught me how to bring computer technology into my teaching; to Nancy Golden, who helped me establish myself as a workshop presenter; to Rick Posner, dear friend, advocate of youth, and keeper of the faith; and to all the teachers who have attended my workshops, who took my ideas and improved upon them to the benefit of their students. I also thank my first publisher, and now longtime friend, Herb Hrebic of the Stack the Deck Writing Program, and Frank Koontz, my mentor, presentation coach, and friend, of the Bureau of Education and Research. Most especially I acknowledge Dorothy Syfert, my teaching partner for the past five years, whose talent in teaching is equaled only by her gifts of dedication, creativity, and compassion. This book would not have been written without her ideas.

—Larry Lewin

In over 33 years of teaching I have had the privilege of meeting and working with many gifted teachers. In particular, I thank Martha Harris, Barbara Shirk, Betsy Shepard, Bill Kentta, and Nancy McCullum for their profound influence on my teaching, for helping me see and develop my own gifts, and for the opportunities to assume leadership in teaching teachers.

—Betty Jean Shoemaker

1 Great Performances: Our Journey Begins

- ➤ Our journey begins
- ➤ An integrated model
- ➤ An introduction to assessment
- ➤ The book as a whole

Do You Recognize This Place?

Betty's Sad Story:

As someone who takes pride in my oral reading skills, I attempt to read in a dramatic way that engages the entire class with the text. On this occasion, I was reading *Charlotte's Web* (White, 1952) to my combined 1st and 2nd grade class. As I neared the end of this popular book, my voice deepened and my words became dignified, "Suddenly a voice was heard on the loudspeaker. 'Attention, please!' it said. `Will Mr. Homer Zuckerman bring his famous pig to the judges' booth in front of the grandstand. A special award will be made there in 20 minutes.'"

One of my freckle-faced 1st graders looked quizzically at me and asked, "You mean Wilbur's the pig? I thought Charlotte was the pig!"

Larry's Sadder Story:

During the debriefing of our three-week in-depth study of Jamestown Colony in the early 1600s, an 8th grader in my U. S. history/language arts class raised her hand and stated,

> I feel like I really get it all now, about Jamestown, and the English colonists coming over on the ships, and trying to survive during the "Starving Time." And the Pocahontas-John Smith thing—you know, the argument over if they had a romance and if she really saved his life. I get all that, but one thing: Was Lincoln still the President back then?

Betty's Saddest Story:

A few years ago I was concerned that my 4th and 5th graders were consistently using stereotypical language to refer to people of color. This concern led me to develop and teach a six-week unit with the goal of unlearning stereotypes about Native Americans, Asian Americans, and Hispanics/Latinos. Students read widely from multiple perspectives, analyzed representations of people of color in the media, and interacted with Asian, Hispanic/Latino, and Native American guests in the classroom. At the end of the unit, we invited a local Native American community leader to class. "What do you know about Native Americans?" this leader asked students. One 10-year-old politely raised her hand, was called on, and earnestly replied: "They kill people."

We would like to begin this book by telling you that the above stories are true: we were there. We recognize this place. This is a place some of you may recognize also. It is a place where teachers are sometimes astounded by how little we know about what our students don't know. From here we set out on a journey. This journey has led us to embrace an integrated approach to curriculum and assessment that makes sense and works for us in the classroom. But let us not get ahead of ourselves: first things first.

Our Journey Begins

We began our journey by looking for a better way to assess our students' acquisition of content knowledge. In the past we typically conducted our assessments at the end of our units or courses. We used mostly paper-and-pencil kinds of assessments found in the teachers' guides of adopted textbooks. We also incorporated culminating projects into our units, but generally as celebratory events for students to showcase their work with little evaluation. We all felt really good about them, but did we really know who learned what? So when we were honest with ourselves, we admitted that we operated under the maxim: I taught; therefore, they learned!

The more we talked about what we wanted to do, the more we began to develop our own notions that challenged the prevailing teaching and learning practices of which we had become a part. These ideas can be summarized as follows:

1. Instead of short "canned" units, we want to teach "meaty" units, where in-depth study takes place and students gain a grasp of major conceptual ideas.

2. In spite of our best attempts, we still have trouble helping students comprehend basic core knowledge facts, concepts, and generalizations. We want to teach in such a way that students really "get it."

3. We cannot assume that all students coming into our classes have the skills needed to process the important content information we are teaching.

4. We are concerned that moving to a standards-based system (as many states are doing) will compel teachers to teach to a narrow band of targets and students to produce the answers they think teachers want.

5. We want to incorporate the newer, more time-consuming performance assessment methods (while continuing to use some traditional methods), but we wrestle with how to pull off the logistics in the classroom.

6. We must expand the opportunities for our student to show what they have learned through various modes, not always paper-and-pencil activities.

7. Our repertoire of assessment strategies needs to include a range of evaluations: from short and specific to lengthy and substantive.

8. Our assessments must arise naturally out of our teaching. They cannot be awkward add-ons to the units or, even worse, irrelevant assessments imposed from the outside.

9. We want to have confidence that how we teach students and assess their work actually contributes to their achievement.

10. We want to embrace methods that assess student work not only at the end of the unit, but also at the beginning and middle.

We know that we are not alone. Many of our colleagues also share these beliefs. Using them as guideposts, we will lead you on a journey through the world of classroom-based assessments. We will share what we've learned about developing performance tasks that measure students' understandings of the content matter we teach them daily in our classrooms. And we promise to be honest with you. Our focus is on the practical, the doable. You can learn from our mistakes. When we as colleagues share with one another, we all improve our abilities to design and elicit "Great Performances" from our students.

To help you better understand the assessment procedures we will be describing in this book, let's briefly look at the integrative model from which they come.

The Coin Model: What Do We Teach?

It doesn't matter whether we teach kindergarten or high school, science or language arts, in urban or rural environments. We all teach two things: knowledge and know-how—sometimes called content and skills. We teach core knowledge content to our students, such as the seasons as a cycle, the separation of powers in the United States Constitution, and facts about the cardiovascular system. And we also teach them key skills, strategies, and processes such as how to read, write, and problem solve.

To help you understand this idea of teaching and assessing these two different kinds of knowledge, we use the metaphor of a coin (Shoemaker and Lewin, 1993). (See fig. 1.)

One face of the coin represents curriculum and the other face assessment. Curriculum and assessment, like the two faces of a coin, are inseparably fused and directly related to each other.

Visualize the coin cut down the center into two interlocking puzzle pieces. One piece describes the "what" of the curriculum, core conceptual knowledge—which most folks call "content." The other piece describes the "know-how" of the curriculum—strategic processes—which most folks simply call "skills." In our model, we define

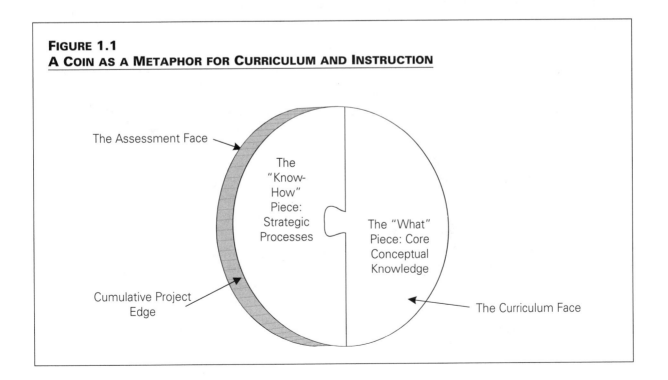

FIGURE 1.1
A COIN AS A METAPHOR FOR CURRICULUM AND INSTRUCTION

The Assessment Face

The "Know-How" Piece: Strategic Processes

The "What" Piece: Core Conceptual Knowledge

Cumulative Project Edge

The Curriculum Face

core knowledge, sometimes referred to as declarative knowledge (Marzano, 1994), as "meaty" conceptual ideas, as opposed to rote factual knowledge. A strategic process, sometimes called procedural knowledge, is a set or a series of interconnected actions that combine skills and/or strategies to produce a particular result or condition—such as comprehending a difficult passage of a book or problem solving to construct a toothpick bridge.

So we teach and assess both pieces of the coin, the acquisition and application of core conceptual knowledge and strategic processes. And in the same way that we model, shape, and routinize the use of any given process, we also help students tap their existing knowledge, refine it, and extend it. Thus, teachers need to assess students' core knowledge understandings at the beginning of the unit, during the unit, and at the end of the unit.

Our coin is three dimensional. Its edge holds the two pieces, content and process, together and melds the assessment face to the curriculum face. This edge represents cumulative projects that students complete at the end of a unit or course. As they complete these projects, students are expected to (1) demonstrate their understanding of key conceptual ideas (content), and (2) apply the strategic processes (skills) taught in the unit or course. Culminating projects are orchestrated efforts to apply core conceptual understandings and strategic processes to create personally meaningful new knowledge.

Let's look closer at the assessment face.

An Introduction to Assessment

Strong assessment systems incorporate four critical elements:

1. Validations emerge from adult judgments about whether a student has met or exceeded the performance standard. They are based on a number of data sources, including direct observations, performances on tasks, student self-assessments, tests, and traditional classroom work. They reflect performance over time.

2. Secured assessments are administered under controlled conditions (during a certain window of time), where no help is given. They may include traditional selected response items and open-ended tasks and are scored outside the classroom environment. Nationally normed standardized tests and state assessment tests are examples of secured assessments.

3. Classroom-embedded assessments arise out of instructional units or courses of study and are administered in the classroom. The four basic types are selected response, essay, performance tasks, and assessments involving direct personal communication with students (Stiggins, 1994). They incorporate the use of uniform, overt scoring systems.

4. Composite records provide evidence of a student's knowledge, skills, and growth over time. They may include actual work samples, scoring guides, self-assessments—or, instead, representations of the work, summaries of scores assigned, and validations, for example.

Classroom Assessments with Overt Scoring Systems

As teachers we use all four of the assessment elements just described. However, it is the third for which we are most directly responsible. We create classroom assessments. We rely upon them far more than the other elements. And we know that we need to do a better job working with them.

As just noted, Stiggins (1994) suggests that classroom assessments take four basic forms. Here's how we understand the four types:

1. Selected response assessments are traditional paper-and-pencil tasks in which the teacher selects the questions and students must respond. A student picks from multiple choices or true/false items, matches items, and fills in short answers.

2. Essay assessments require a student to produce a longer written response to a teacher prompt.

3. Performance assessments call for the student to construct a response within a context. Popular performance tasks include storywriting, science lab experiments, and debates. Evaluation criteria are clearly identified in the form of dimensions or traits, and the focus of evaluation is on both the product and the process used to produce it.

4. Personal communications as assessment include substantive dialogue during instruction, interviews, conferences, conversations, and oral examinations.

In this book we are going to zero in on the third type, performance assessments. Why? Because they work for us. They allow us to assess content and process simultaneously. They are more engaging for students. They give us feedback that helps us improve our instruction.

And now the big question: Just what exactly are *performance assessments*? Performance assessments encompass a range from short and specific to lengthy and substantive; from *mini,* which open a window into a student's developmental thinking early in a unit, to *maxi,* which paint a picture of a student's overall thinking at the end of the unit. Performance tasks fall within this broad range.

In our definition, a performance *task* has the following key characteristics:

- Students have some choice in selecting or shaping the task.
- The task requires both the elaboration of core knowledge content and the use of key processes.

- The task has an explicit scoring system.
- The task is designed for an audience larger than the teacher, that is, others outside the classroom would find value in the work.
- The task is carefully crafted to measure what it purports to measure.

In summary, a performance task can be completed in different lengths of time: in one class period—a *mini;* in two or three class periods—a *midi;* or a more substantive task taking a week or more to complete—a *maxi.*

Snapshot of Chapter 1

In this chapter we provided a big-picture overview of why we set out on our assessment journey. We told you the 10 key notions we used to develop our new assessments, as well as the central elements of our integrative model: content and process. We also explored the four essential elements of a strong assessment program and four types of classroom-based assessments.

At this point, you may want to take a few minutes and jot down your reflections on this chapter. Here are some questions to consider:

- What did I learn that I might use in my classroom?
- What information included here might help me with my teaching and assessment?
- What am I going to take with me from this chapter on my own assessment journey?
- What questions do I have that I want to explore soon?

We are interested in a continuing dialogue with teachers on this journey. Please share your thoughts and reactions with us.

A Preview of Coming Attractions

In the chapters that follow we offer a close-up look at our view of classroom-based assessments—the assessment face of our coin.

In Chapter 2, we provide you with background on how students acquire content knowledge—*Info In*—using the key learning processes of reading, listening, manipulating, and viewing. We also introduce the *Prepare, First Dare, Repair, and Share* universal approach to teaching these key processes. In addition, we examine the four modes that *Info Out* can take—graphic, written, oral, and constructions. Students use these vehicles to make their content understanding explicit to teachers and other adults for evaluation.

In Chapter 3, we will explore the first Info Out mode, *visual representations*, in which students share their content knowledge through graphic or-

ganizers, comic strips, electronic slide shows, and the like.

In Chapters 4, 5, and 6 respectively, we examine three additional Info Out modes: *writing* (for example, a historical persuasive letter and a parent advisory brochure); *oral presentations* (such as round-robin mini-speeches and debates); and *large-scale substantive projects/performances* (including museum exhibits and models and prototypes.

In the final chapter, we summarize several strengths and weaknesses of classroom-based performance assessments.

In particular, we want to share performance tasks that we have designed and used with students as an integral part of an existing unit or course of study. These tasks vary in length and complexity and take various forms. They can be used as assessments at the beginning of the unit, during the unit, and at the end of the unit.

2 Info In: How Students Learn New Content Information

➤ An overview of Info In
➤ A four-step process approach
➤ Info In through viewing
➤ Info In through hands-on manipulating

Larry's Story

At the end of a unit on Colonial American history, a class of 8th graders asked their teacher if he would rent the Disney video *Pocahontas* and show it in class. Knowing it was a long shot, they bolstered their brash request with the following arguments:

• They had been studying Colonial American history for "over *three* weeks."
• They had focused on the Jamestown Colony.
• They had studied Captain John Smith.
• They had learned about the powerful Powhatan tribe, whose most famous member was, and still is, none other than Pocahontas.

As pleased as they were with this rationale, they were shocked at how quickly their teacher agreed. The wily old fox, Larry, quickly hatched a plan of his own. Instead of automatically rejecting their request, I seized the teachable moment. Here

was a golden opportunity to teach my students how to analyze U.S. history critically, which is a major goal of the class.

"Okay," I said, "but here's the deal: I will only show a commercial video in class if it clearly has an educational purpose. I'll show the Disney video if, after viewing it, you agree to analyze the accuracy of its historical content." I smiled inwardly at my cleverness. Then it was their turn to shock me.

"Sure!" they cried.

"Why not?"

"We'd be honored to."

And one very eager student offered, "Mr. Lewin, you know that we want to do very well on this, so we'd like to get started as soon as possible. Could we begin by watching *Pocahontas* RIGHT NOW?"

The next day I went to my neighborhood video store and rented *Pocahontas*. Over the next couple of days my 8th graders watched it with an analytical eye.

This was not the first time these students were expected to analyze history critically. This ability was a major outcome for my class as well as classes across the state. Social science analysis is one key learning standard from the State of Oregon's curriculum: "Design and implement strategies to analyze issues, explain perspectives, and resolve issues using the social sciences" (Oregon Department of Education, 1998).

I had worked with my students to identify bias in historical sources, to evaluate an author's credentials, and to compare primary and secondary sources. And, in particular, throughout the entire year I gave them repeated opportunities to analyze events from various perspectives.

Because both my students and I knew that this ability to present a historical analysis was a goal, a state standard, I needed to ensure that they knew how to do it. To succeed in their analysis of the *Pocahontas* video, they first needed to learn basic factual knowledge (concepts) about the topic. We call methods of acquiring this basic core knowledge "Info In."

Info In: Learning New Content

Students take in important content information on Colonial American history, or any other topic of study, in four ways:

- Reading
- Listening
- Manipulating/using hands-on activities
- Viewing/Observing

Therefore, to learn about Jamestown and Pocahontas, my students could *read* books, articles, or primary source documents; *listen* to me or an invited expert speak about the subject; participate in a *hands-on* experience related to the event; or *view* a video, slideshow, or film about it.

We call these processes the four Info In modes. So during the study of the Jamestown Colony, I consciously used all four of these modes. I assigned readings, lectured (briefly), had my students construct a model of a Jamestown temporary shelter, and showed them videos, including their favorite, Disney's *Pocahontas*.

Let's be clear about where we are headed. Before addressing how we assess student learning of content, we must first consider how they learn that content. The purposes of this chapter are

- To introduce you to Info In: how learners use key learning processes to acquire content knowledge
- To show you how we teach Info In processes to students

Of the four Info In modes, we have chosen to focus on viewing and manipulating in this chapter for four important reasons:

1. Video viewing and hands-on manipulating are increasingly popular in our schools.
2. Students often misperceive both video viewing and hands-on learning time as kick-back, do-nothing time.
3. Teachers typically don't instruct students on how to effectively watch videos and/or participate in hands-on activities.
4. The unfortunate results are often either widespread boredom or, worse, the potential for mass chaos.

First, let's illustrate how Larry's middle school class applied the viewing process to actively gain expertise about the historical relationships between Native American peoples and the first English colonists. Then we will follow with Betty's elementary-level example of using manipulatives in a science experiment to help students gain expertise about the transmission of germs.

The Viewing Process: From Larry's Middle Grades Perspective

As a classroom teacher, I (Larry) have observed that too many students do not maximize Info In while watching a video. They just don't know how to process new content information through viewing. Likewise, I cannot assume that they all know how to read successfully, listen attentively, or even use kinesthetic manipulations to learn new content. Because of a variety of in- and out-of-school factors, too many students are unable to effectively apply these processes to take in new information.

Therefore, it's my job to teach them how to skillfully read, listen, manipulate, and view. To teach learners how to Info In through these modes, I use a generic four-step process approach: *Prepare, First Dare, Repair,* and *Share.* These four steps rhyme to help students remember them. We have trained teachers in our district, in our state, and across the country to use this approach to successfully teach learners in the primary grades, intermediate grades, middle school, and high school.

Prepare means to get ready to process new information. *First Dare* is a learner's first attempt to access that new information. *Repair* recognizes the need to return to the information in order to fine-tune or upgrade the initial (the First Dare) understanding. And last, *Share* allows the learner to reveal what he or she has learned.

Before I rolled the Disney *Pocahontas* video, I asked myself, What would a good viewer do to Prepare for successful viewing to bring in new content knowledge about this topic? Most students would answer something like "get comfortable" or "get food." Good preparation involves more than physical comfort. It involves mental readiness. An active, engaged viewer establishes some mental mechanism through which to incorporate new content information into his or her existing knowledge base. You might say it is like constructing a mental hat rack on which to hang the upcoming new information.

But how many students know how to mentally get ready for viewing? For most 8th graders, video readiness typically meant trying to sit next to a best friend or hunkering down for an opportune nap in the darkened classroom without threat of teacher interrogation.

To Prepare for the video viewing, I had the class construct a three-columned wall chart on "What we already know about Jamestown, John Smith, and Pocahontas." I called on volunteers and nonvolunteers alike to share what they had in their heads about these three related topics. I recorded this information on the butcher paper wall chart. This activity tapped prior knowledge, which we know is critical to incorporating new information into preexisting mental categories. Of course, a clever teacher could require each student to individually complete this task first before using it with the whole class. How might this be done?

I invented the "Folded File Folder" (FFF) activity for this purpose. Playing off the metaphor of file folders for the mental categories humans create in their memories, the FFF teaches students some important comprehension strategies. I distributed 8½-by-11-inch papers (colored paper, to get their attention) and asked them to fold them in half leaving a ½- to 1-inch tab on top (see fig. 2.1).

After labeling the tab with the topic about to be viewed—in this case, Colonial America—students opened the Folded File Folder and used the top inside section (between the tab and fold) to create three columns. At the top of each column they added a subtitle: Jamestown Colony, Captain John Smith, and Pocahontas. I next asked my students to tap their prior knowledge of each subtitle by jotting down anything they already knew, or thought they knew. I told them, "Tapping prior knowledge is a key strategy for synthesizing new information while viewing a video."

One more preparation: I instructed them to quickly predict what they thought the video might tell them. They recorded their predictions in the middle of the FFF—writing across the center fold.

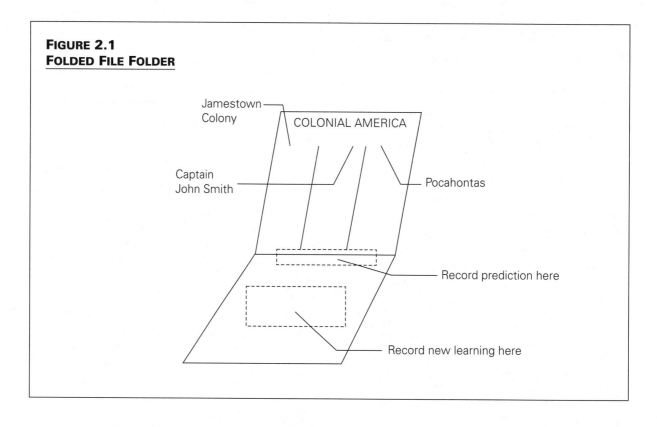

FIGURE 2.1
FOLDED FILE FOLDER

(Because some students were hesitant to mispredict, I assured them that there is no such a thing as a "bad" prediction.) This strategy of prediction is very important for successful comprehension building and could be added to the class wall chart. The bottom portion of the FFF is reserved for taking notes on new information "Info In-ed" during the viewing that fosters active viewing.

As an alternative, the next time I teach this particular content information, I may try a different prior knowledge tapper. The students could make a Pocahontas Picture Postcard, on a 5" x 8" index card. (See Chapter 4, p. 75, for a description of this activity.)

So three effective Prepare strategies include (1) a class wall chart, (2) an individual Folded File Folder, and (3) a Picture Postcard. While I used these strategies in an American history class at the middle level, they can be easily adapted for use at

other levels, with other subjects, and with the other Info In processes of reading, listening, and manipulating.

The First Dare: Roll That Video

Before I could play the video for my eager audience, I had to consider, What do good viewers need to do to remain engaged, alert, and active constructors of meaning during the First Dare viewing?

One answer is to require them to take notes while viewing. Do your students respond less than appreciatively when you tell them to take notes? Using the bottom half of the FFF for note taking is a nonintimidating strategy because of the small amount of room provided. Framing the task as, "Jot down any interesting information," as opposed to "Take notes," also reduces intimidation. Go-getters can also use the back of the FFF to continue note taking, draw a picture, or construct a concept map about the information being viewed.

Courtney wrote in her FFF, "I didn't realize how important gold was to the English colonists—they spend a lot of time in this scene looking for gold."

Greg Barnett, a colleague in another Oregon district, adapted our FFF idea for a unit on the solar system. He created the "folded sun" template. On the front side, students listed facts they already knew about the sun and questions they wanted to answer during the study. At the end of the unit, they recorded what they learned on the back. Greg was very pleased with the increased level of attention to the topic—so pleased that he sent us the folded sun shown in Figure 2.2.

As engaging as the Folded File Folder/Folded Sun are, I often use a different First Dare activity with middle grades: the Venn diagram. My students used the Venn to compare and contrast the Disney video with *The Double Life of Pocahontas* by Jean Fritz (1983). This graphic organizer is perfect for comparing and contrasting information in order to comprehend and synthesize it. Because my students had studied Pocahontas earlier in class, they were able to compare information from the video with the knowledge they had acquired from other nonfiction sources. I told them, "Use the right circle of the Venn diagram to record information that you learned from the video. Use the left circle to record information that you learned from reading the biography."

An active listener in the class then asked, "What goes into the middle section?"

I told them to use the middle section of a Venn diagram to record information agreed upon from both sources. The class liked that idea—a rare treat for a middle school teacher!

To ensure active use of the Venn diagram during viewing, I periodically hit the pause button of the VCR's remote control—an idea I borrowed from Dorothy Syfert, my next-door colleague. She stops the video at key places to give her students

time to pause, think, and write. Now I do too. Figure 2.3 shows Navin's Venn diagram—an effective First Dare Strategy—completed by this middle school student.

Alternatively, I have used a third First Dare viewing activity, The Open Mind, which I learned from my friend and colleague, Grace Herr. This graphic organizer is the outline of a person's head, giving the illusion of looking into an open mind (see fig. 2.4, p. 14). Students record (textually and/or graphically) their perceptions of what the person would have been thinking at that moment. By perceiving thoughts in an Open Mind, a student must be *actively* "Info In-ing."

During the video, I periodically hit the pause button of the remote control, and instructed the viewers to fill in the open mind—using text or graphics—with their projections of what might be going on inside the mind of a main character, such as Pocahontas, John Smith, or Chief Wahunsonakok (known throughout history as Chief Powhatan). The Open Mind proved to be an effective Info In device.

Note that the generic process approach I'm describing here usually requires the third step: Repair. Typically students do not Info In adequately during their First Dare attempt. They need another shot at the information to construct meaningful knowledge.

Repairing Initial Understandings

The Prepare and First Dare strategies just discussed—tapping prior knowledge, making predictions, and taking notes through the use of Folded File Folders, Venn diagrams, Picture Postcards, Open Minds, and the like—were effective teaching methods. They also helped me identify the major misconceptions and confusions that students continued to hold. Using that information, I designed several Repair activities to address these misconceptions.

By quickly reviewing the FFFs, I found out which kids knew a lot, knew some, or knew little.

11

FIGURE 2.2
A MIDDLE SCHOOL STUDENT'S FOLDED SUN

THE SUN

(Front)

Things I already
know about the sun:

1. it is round.
2. we rotate around it.
3. it is hot.
4. Don't look at it.

Things I need to know about the sun:

How far from the earth is it?
What kind of gases does it burn on?
How hot can it get?
How long will this unit
last?

THINGS I LEARNED ABOUT THE SUN

(Back)

• The sun is a fusion reactor.
• The sun is the center of the solar system.
• Energy release the suns fuel
layers of the sun.
• Know nucular fusion photospere
layers of the sun weigh of human
on sun (gravity vs. mass)
—activities on sun
(storms, sunspots, prominences).
• solar wind/flares.

Note: To accurately show the student's work, we've left errors uncorrected.

FIGURE 2.3
A MIDDLE SCHOOL STUDENT'S VENN DIAGRAM

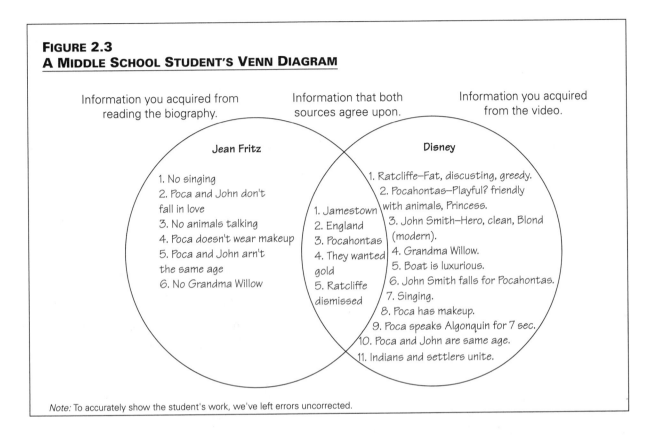

Information you acquired from reading the biography.

Information that both sources agree upon.

Information you acquired from the video.

Jean Fritz

1. No singing
2. Poca and John don't fall in love
3. No animals talking
4. Poca doesn't wear makeup
5. Poca and John arn't the same age
6. No Grandma Willow

1. Jamestown
2. England
3. Pocahontas
4. They wanted gold
5. Ratcliffe dismissed

Disney

1. Ratcliffe—Fat, discusting, greedy.
2. Pocahontas—Playful? friendly with animals, Princess.
3. John Smith—Hero, clean, Blond (modern).
4. Grandma Willow.
5. Boat is luxurious.
6. John Smith falls for Pocahontas.
7. Singing.
8. Poca has makeup.
9. Poca speaks Algonquin for 7 sec.
10. Poca and John are same age.
11. Indians and settlers unite.

Note: To accurately show the student's work, we've left errors uncorrected.

Some of my students had constructed major misinformation about the topic. One boy, for example, had written in his FFF that "Jamestown was built from the wreckage of the Santa Maria." He had obviously confused information from a topic studied earlier in the year. As chagrined as I was, knowing what he was really thinking helped me determine what to address next.

I also collected and evaluated the Open Mind worksheets, which revealed that students embraced certain notions from the video that historians still continue to debate. I could have used the Content Acquisition Developmental Continuum (discussed on pp. 113 and 120, Chapter 6).

So I decided to replay a critical scene from the video using a different version of the Open Mind, the Portrait. Instead of a faceless outline, the Portrait featured a photocopied face from a painting of the real Pocahontas, along with a giant open bubble in which to record thoughts.

As the class reviewed the scene, I paused the tape and asked them, "Based on what you know about the real historical events, what might the *real* Pocahontas, not the cartoon character, have been thinking in this scene?" The results indicated an expanded analysis of the video's version of history (see fig. 2.5, p. 15, for student Christine's work).

So where are we now? We have learned that Prepare-to-view, First Dare viewing, and Repair activities serve both instructional and assessment roles. They help learners access and process new information, and they simultaneously inform the teacher/assessor about the learning that is taking place.

So, at each stage of instruction, I check in with students to determine who is learning what (both conceptions and misconceptions) and to determine at what level they are constructing meaning. We

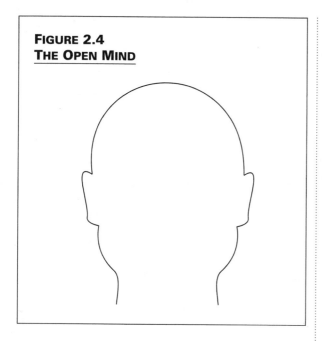

**FIGURE 2.4
THE OPEN MIND**

are committed to assessing content understandings three times:

• *Before* (at the beginning of a unit or course)—examining the Folded File Folders or the Picture Postcards.
• *During* (in the middle of a unit or course)—evaluating the Folded File Folders again, the Open Minds, or the Venn diagrams.
• *After* (as a culmination to a unit or course)—assessing students' historical analyses of the video. (See discussion below.)

Mini-Performance Assessments

Whether I use the Folded File Folder, the Picture Postcard, the Venn diagram, an Open Mind, or the famous K-W-L (Ogle, 1986 [see Chapter 3]), I realize that none of these active-viewing activities qualifies as performance *tasks* because they don't meet our five criteria of performance tasks from Chapter 1. But they are performance *assessments*. They don't qualify as *maxi-* or *midi-performance tasks but are effective mini-*assessment tools. They help learners acquire important con-

tent information, move closer and closer to the targeted outcomes, and simultaneously provide their teachers with important feedback on that learning. They have become a cornerstone of our instruction. In the next four chapters, we will share numerous mini-, midi-, and maxi-performance assessments for use before, during, and at the end of a course of study.

The Maxi-Performance Task

The third opportunity for assessing my students' understanding of the content knowledge comes at the end of the unit or course. We call this fourth step of the process *Share*. It's like raising the curtain for a performance. After weeks of rehearsal (a.k.a. target practice with the mini-assessments), it is now show time—time to demonstrate what you know and what you can do.

How can a student show off what he or she knows and can do? A student uses one of the following four modes that Info Out can take (with examples):

1. *Visual representation:*
• Draw a comic strip
• Make a graphic organizer
• Design a poster or an advertisement
• Construct a computer-generated slide show or HyperStudio® stack

2. *Writing*:
• Write a comparison/contrast essay of the Disney version and the nonfiction version of *Pocahantas* using a Venn diagram
• Write a persuasive letter to the current chief of the Powhatan Nation or to the chair of Disney Studios
•Write a historical fiction short story synthesizing historical fact and imagined fiction

3. *Speaking*:
• Participate in a debate about the two accounts of the events

• Conduct a mock interview with historical figures

   • Recite the tribal history of this event

4. Substantive projects or performances:

   • Act out key historical scenes in a role-play, simulation, or dramatization

   • Construct an accurate model of Jamestown and/or the Powhatan village of Wererocomoco complete with notes

While the fourth mode would have been a crowd pleaser, as a teacher I knew that constructing a model was a difficult way to get at the historical analysis target I had identified. Remember, I expected the class "to analyze the accuracy of the historical content of the video *Pocahontas.*" How would building a model of the English colony or the Powhatan village accomplish this? Because I had tried this hands-on task in past years, I realized it did not.

So, I picked the written mode and I assigned students the maxi-performance task of composing a persuasive letter arguing their opinion about the video. They could choose the recipient. (We describe this written performance task in Chapter 4.)

These four Info Out modes allow students to demonstrate their content knowledge construction. After studying content throughout the unit, using all four Info In modes, they should have gained a degree of expertise. The students clearly believed they had. Here are some quotes from their persuasive letters:

> I'm an 8th grader at Monroe Middle School. We have been studying Pocahontas for quite some time (a long time!), so I've become an *expert on the situation.*

> My classmates and I in our block class have studied a lot on Pocahontas, Jamestown, and even John Smith, so I feel *I know what I'm talking about.*

FIGURE 2.5
A MIDDLE SCHOOL STUDENT'S PORTRAIT

The Real Pocahontas

1. I like him.
2. Thank Goodness I saved him in time or else he would have been killed.
3. Father will let him go.
4. Now he will be my brother.
5. I'm so happy we might create piece.

What might the real Pocahontas have been thinking in this scene?

Source of image: The Library of Virginia

Note: To accurately show the student's work, we've left errors uncorrected.

I am an *expert of sorts* on the subject. I have read books about her and have seen a documentary on her life.

[To Roy Disney, Vice Chairman, Disney Studios] I believe I *know a lot about* Pocahontas. In fact it seems as if I have learned more in a month than you have learned in your life. Thank you. Have a nice day.

The Manipulating Process: From Betty's Primary Grade Perspective

Next let's explore how to use the generic process approach—Prepare, First Dare, Repair, and Share—to teach young students to take in information through hands-on manipulation activities. As an example, I (Betty) will show you how I taught elementary students to conduct a typical scientific investigation.

The formal scientific process, we should note, is the "granddaddy" of process approaches. From this centuries-old scientific method come other process approaches including our generic four-step approach. Figure 2.6 shows this relationship.

What we are saying is that you really can teach the process approach—whether it is scientific investigation, writing, reading, viewing, oral presenting, or problem solving—using Prepare, First Dare, Repair, and Share. But can it be done successfully with 1st and 2nd graders?

Our district's content standards for health include:

Knows essential concepts about the prevention and control of communicable and noncommunicable diseases

For Grade 3, the benchmark expectations are:

• Knows signs and symptoms of common diseases and how to prevent them

• Knows ways to prevent or reduce the risk of disease

• Knows and practices good self-care

Because of my interest in teaching young students the formal scientific method in such a way as to involve them in a hands-on activity, I developed a unit titled, "How to Catch a Cold."

Prepare: Becoming Disease Detectives

At the time, a number of my students had been out with colds and flu. Several were just returning after missing several days. "What is causing this cold and flu epidemic?" I asked the class on the first day of the unit.

Nearly in unison, students proclaimed, "Germs!"

I responded, "What are germs? Where can we find germs? How can we find them? I can't see any around here? How do we know germs are around us?"

Looking puzzled, several students attempted to explain: "You can't see them. They are too tiny to be seen. But they are here." After a few minutes of probing, one student volunteered that a doctor had used a swab to scrape germs out of his throat and then rubbed the swab into a little plastic dish. He didn't know any more about the process, but he knew that doctors did those kinds of things.

I then took the class to the boys' and girls' rest rooms and asked them to read the prominently displayed signs by the sinks, "Hand washing prevents infection." I asked,"Is that true? What does hand washing have to do with germs? Can we prove that this statement is true?"

Back in class, I introduced students to the formal scientific method through an activity I called "Let's Investigate: Disease Detectives." I walked them through the following directions:

In the next week we will all become special scientists called *epidemiologists*—scientists who study diseases—especially contagious ones that affect communities. Epidemiologists use the scientific method to uncover the causes of infectious diseases, and they teach people in a community how to prevent the spread of germs that cause diseases

FIGURE 2.6
COMPARING *PREPARE*, *FIRST DARE*, *REPAIR*, AND *SHARE* WITH OTHER PROCESS APPROACHES

Our Four-Step Process Approach	The Formal Scientific Method	The Writing Process
1. **Prepare**: Get ready to process new information.	1. State the problem and form a hypothesis.	1. Prewriting.
2. **First Dare**: Try out something and begin to make sense of it.	2. Observe and experiment.	2. Drafting.
3. **Repair**: Return to the information, improve on your initial understanding.	3. Interpret data. Identify variables. Re-experiment.	3. Revising and editing.
4. **Share**: Share what you have learned.	4. Draw and state conclusions.	4. Publishing a final draft.

like strep throat and flu. How do epidemiologists approach their work? They use the process approach!

Next I explained the steps:

1. They *Prepare*: Epidemiologists identify a problem. They ask questions. They think about what they already know about the topic. They come up with a possible explanation.

2. They *First Dare*: Epidemiologists set up experiments and observe what happens.

3. They *Repair*: Epidemiologists study the data: the information they obtain from the experiment. Then they rerun the experiment to make sure they have considered all of the important factors that might affect their results.

4. They *Share*: Epidemiologists pull together their research and share what they have learned with others—usually by writing a paper about their work.

Before I taught this unit, the district's Assessment Task Force (Eugene Public School District 4J, 1995), developed a list of Prepare, First Dare, Repair, and Share strategies that scientists would likely use to conduct a scientific investigation. After setting up the simulation using the above process, I gave each student a copy of the following

menu of strategies to improve their use of the scientific investigation process:

*1. Prepare: How well do I **prepare** to do a scientific investigation?*

a. I know why I am doing this experiment and what I want to find out.

b. I think about everything I already know about this topic.

c. I gather the equipment and materials I need to do the experiment.

d. I get help from others if needed.

e. I make a hypothesis and set up an experiment to test it.

*2. First Dare: How well do I handle the **beginning work** on a scientific investigation?*

a. I conduct an experiment.

b. I observe and record what happens.

c. I see if my experiment proved or disproved my hypothesis.

*3. Repair: How well do I use **revising** strategies to improve my scientific investigation?*

a. I make a new hypothesis if appropriate.

b. I redo the experiment.

c. I record the results.

d. I check for any mistakes.

4. Share: *How well do I **share** the results of my scientific investigation?*

    a. I present my results to others.

    b. I listen to comments.

    c. I compare my findings with those of others who did the same experiment.

    d. I think about another experiment I might do.

To continue to Prepare for our study, the class discussed what we thought we knew about germs. Following our discussion, each student constructed a Scrapbook in which to record his or her thoughts, using a combination of pictures and labels. Scrapbooks are one more technique for tapping prior knowledge, like the Folded File Folder for older students described earlier in this chapter.

You can introduce the use of a Scrapbook by sharing a photo album of a personal trip. Remind students that one constructs a Scrapbook before, during, and/or after a trip as a way to remember special experiences from the journey. In this case, ask students to begin constructing a Scrapbook of what they think they know about germs—anything that comes to mind. Throughout the unit they will add new learnings based on their experiences.

Info In Via the Listening Mode

On day two, to further Prepare for our scientific investigation, we invited a local health care professional to the classroom to discuss bacteria and viruses and how they are spread. She walked students through the process of taking a throat culture, explaining what doctors use as a medium in which to grow bacteria. She pointed out that viruses, bacteria, and fungi can be grown in what epidemiologists call petri dishes.

On day three I set up stations in the classroom staffed by high school science and visual art students from our nearby high school. I personally worked with students at station four. The groups and their focus of study included:

- *Station One:* What can we learn about germs?
- *Station Two:* How can we use a microscope to view bacteria and fungi?
- *Station Three:* How can we keep track of our data through observational drawings?
- *Station Four:* How do we ask questions and form hypotheses?
- *Station Five:* How can we keep track of our data with charts and graphs?

Students rotated from station to station during one afternoon. They spent about 25 minutes at each station and participated in hands-on activities at each.

The following day, as we continued to Prepare to move into the First Dare stage, I gave the class a list of questions generated at station four. We agreed as a class to pursue the question, "Does hand washing prevent infection?" Question asking is an excellent prepare-to-learn strategy. We developed the following hypothesis:

> Washing your hands will remove most of the germs from your hands. If this is true, then fewer germs will grow in the petri dishes of students who have washed their hands.

We also completed another manipulative activity—one that I borrowed from my friend, Barbara Shirk, a teacher at Eugene's Patterson Family School. I devised a way to use it to involve students in learning key content using a hands-on approach. Students constructed an origami "fortune teller," the perennial childhood folded paper toy. They then recorded basic information on each flap (the importance of hand washing, how germs are transmitted, etc.). My students then taught other students at school the basics of hand washing.

First Dare: Is Our Hypothesis True?

We used the same method that medical personnel use to grow germs from throat cultures. A local medical laboratory donated 60 prepared petri dishes for our project. I didn't mind the heartburn from gobbling my lunch in the car as I sped over to pick them up.

On day four, we started the experiment after morning recess. We formed four experimental groups:

Group One: One third of the class did not wash their hands.

Group Two: One third of the class washed their hands with cold water and no soap.

Group Three: One third of the class washed their hands with hot water and antibacterial soap.

Group Four: Eight teachers we selected at random who did not know about our hypothesis (to prevent extra hand washing).

Each student labeled the top of one petri dish with his or her name and with "washed-hot and soap," "washed-cold, no soap," or "not washed." Everyone was careful not to lift the lids. After washers washed their hands, all groups carefully lifted their lids and tapped the ball of the fingers of one hand onto the nutrient agar pre-poured in the bottom of the dishes. Lids were closed, taped shut, and placed on the counter by the sink. A few students then went around to other classrooms and asked certain teachers to touch one hand in the petri dish. They labeled these dishes "Teacher a, b, c, and so forth." Next they asked those teachers how recently they had washed their hands with soap and water. The students recorded these times on the lids of the dishes as well.

Back in the classroom, students finished their first observational drawings of the experiment. Each student completed a drawing of his or her own dish plus one dish from another group for their Scrapbooks. This important recording of "information coming in" mirrors the use of Venn diagramming while viewing a video in the middle grade history classroom described earlier. (See Larry's example starting on page 9.)

Right before the end of the school day, students completed another observational drawing of the same dishes. At the same time on each following day, they drew observations of the same dishes. I encouraged my students to write any comments they deemed appropriate. Figure 2.7 shows one student's observational drawing.

Share: The Results

Wait! What happened to Repair? I deliberately skipped it this time and went straight to Share. Just remember that the generic template is recursive: you can move easily forward and backward as needed, in and out of stages. The better you get at the process, the more easily and efficiently you will move through the stages.

And, sometimes, depending on your proficiency, you can skip a stage all together. For example, if I tried to fix plumbing by myself, believe me, I would labor through each stage of the process due to my lack of plumbing problem-solving experience. A plumber, however, could move much more efficiently from stage to stage–maybe even skipping or abbreviating a stage!

So, in the afternoon of day three, we all gathered around the petri dishes and observed various colonies of bacteria and fungi. We listed our findings on chart paper. As you can predict, the hand washers' dishes were clearer than those of nonwashers. Students chose from the listed phrases on the chart paper to craft their own conclusions, which they recorded and placed in their Scrapbooks. I instructed them to start with

• Our hypothesis was . . .
• This experiment proved our hypothesis to be true/untrue for these reasons . . .
• I continue to have questions about . . .

Back to Repair: Reruns

The cultures in some dishes, however, seemed to support a different conclusion. Bacteria were growing in dishes where hand washing had occurred—not to the extent of the nonwashers, but enough to make one wonder. I took this opportunity to introduce the notion of Repair.

I suggested that there must have been something else going on in those dishes. We hypothesized what that might be. I added to the student variable list and instructed students to partner with a classmate to redo the experiment (Repair) controlling for one of the following variables:

• Hands with long fingernails and hands with short fingernails

• Hands washed in cold water and hands washed in hot water

• Hands washed for 30 seconds and hands washed for two minutes

• Hands on which someone had recently coughed and hands that had been in one's mouth

• Hands recently run through hair or hands rubbed over clothing

• Petri dishes stored in a dark, moist place and those stored in a dry, bright place

You may be able to think of other variables you would like to add to this list. My directions are shown in Figure 2.8.

Share: Working with Each Team

Each team was expected to bring its Scrapbook to an interview with me. Of course, I used other Info Out options (for example, graphic representations, observational drawings) and written descriptions. I chose to add the oral option, interviewing, because of its developmental appropriateness for 1st and 2nd graders.

FIGURE 2.7
DOES HAND WASHING PREVENT INFECTION? A 2ND GRADER'S OBSERVATIONAL DRAWING

Name: Ruby
Date: March 17 97   Time: 10:30

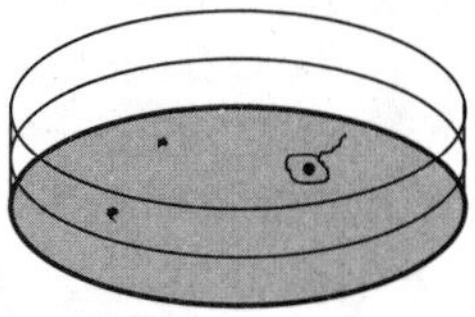

My dish: Miles   's dish:

I see: Slimy stuff. And white spots.   I see: Cracks and white spots.

Brown stuff.   Gooey gunky stuff

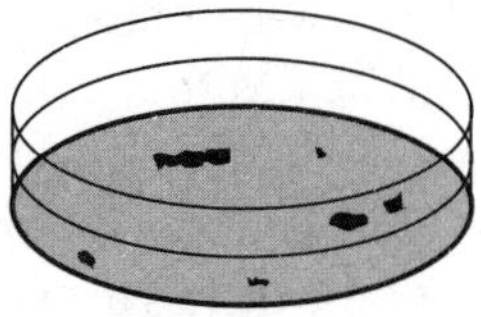

For each interview, I used Piaget's clinical interview format[1] to review the work of the team. I asked the following questions:

- What variables did you decide to study?
- What was your hypothesis?
- How did you conduct your experiment?
- What were your results?
- Did anyone else in the class study the same variables, and were their results similar?

----

[1]H. Ginsburg and S. Opper, (1988), *Piaget's theory of intellectual development,* (Englewood Cliffs, NJ: Prentice Hall).

- What questions do you still have?
- What gives you confidence that your work is accurate?

As I conferenced with students, I evaluated their work using the simplified scientific investigation scoring guide in Figure 2.9.

Of course, my description has been a "bullet train" journey through the How to Catch a Cold unit. We did a number of other Info In activities to develop concepts and teach the use of the key scientific investigation strategies. Because of the developmental level of students, we did not go into

---

FIGURE 2.8
FOLLOW-UP HAND-WASHING EXPERIMENT: CONTROLLING FOR VARIABLES

Partner Names _____ and _____

Follow this process, step by step. Keep this form in your "Scrapbook." Put your initials in the box on the left when you have completed each step of the scientific investigation process.

Initial Here:	Step	Do This:
	Prepare	1. Write both of your names on the outside of a manila folder. This is your team "Scrapbook." 2. Pick a variable that you intend to experiment with. Write it on the front cover of your album. 3. What do you think you will find after running your experiment? Develop a hypothesis, and record it on the front cover of your album. 4. Gather your materials. You will need two petri dishes. 5. Label the dishes. 6. Review the scoring guide. That is how your work will be scored.
	First Dare	1. Begin your experiment. Complete a drawing of your work, and date the drawing worksheet. 2. Complete another observational drawing right before you go home today. Put both drawings in your Scrapbook.
	Repair	1. Check to see if anything unusual is happening. 2. Complete another observational drawing.
	Share	1. Complete your last observational drawing. 2. Complete the worksheet titled "Sharing Our Results." 3. Be prepared to share your results with the class.

all of the variables that could influence what appears in the petri dishes. Instead, we narrowed our focus to those that students at this level would understand.

As a culmination to the Share stage, the class generated a list of key factors that contributed to or inhibited the spread of bacteria and viruses. From that list, each student created his or her own humorous pop-up book illustrating how these factors contribute to catching a cold. Students were highly motivated by this Info Out activity—being able to share their content expertise with others.

Next time I'm going to have students work individually and then as a group to create several news articles for a class newspaper on this project. (See Chapter 4.)

I should also note that for each key process we teach, we have generated a menu of strategies just like the ones listed for the scientific investigation process. We teach these strategies explicitly to students. Having a large repertoire of strategies to use at any given stage in a process makes for good readers, writers, scientific problem solvers!

So, How to Catch a Cold is our example of teaching the hands-on manipulating mode of Info In using scientific investigation and the Prepare, First Dare, Repair, and Share process in which students literally had a *hands-on* experience!

FIGURE 2.9
SCIENTIFIC INVESTIGATION SCORING GUIDE

Name _____   Date _____

Score	Trait
1 2 3 4	We developed a hypothesis.
1 2 3 4	We tested our hypothesis in an experiment.
1 2 3 4	We interpreted our data.
1 2 3 4	We stated our conclusions.

1 = Not present: We did not do this.
2 = Beginning Work: We did this, but it looks like the work of a beginner.
3 = Progressing Work: Our work is fine in this area.
4 = Accomplished Work: Our work shows that we developed this trait very well.

Comments: _____

_____

_____

_____

_____

Snapshot of Chapter 2

In this chapter we

• Introduced you to Info In: the use of key learning processes of reading, viewing, listening, and manipulating to acquire content knowledge

• Shared our generic template—Prepare, First Dare, Repair, and Share—for teaching the process approach to students of all ages

• Gave you two unit examples, one at the middle level and one at the primary level.

Take a few minutes to jot down your reflections on this chapter. What information included here might help you with your teaching and assessing. Does this information make sense? How might you adapt it to your setting?

As we have explained, the fourth stage of our four-step process approach is Share. As teachers we may teach our students four different modes of sharing to reveal what they've learned. In this chapter we have referred to them as creating graphic representations, writing, speaking, and constructing models and performances. In the following four chapters, we will go into each of these different modes in great detail.

3 Info Out: Assessing Students' Understanding with Visual Representations

> ➤ An introduction to Info Out through the use of graphic tools
> ➤ Assessment before, during, and after units and courses
> ➤ The world's first *ChecBric*

Larry's Story

An 8th grade language arts/U.S. history class was shocked to learn that Christopher Columbus's flagship, the Santa Maria, had cracked open its hull and started to sink off the coast of the Caribbean island Bohio. The students acquired this little known historical fact by reading their history textbook's account of the events in 1492, (fig. 3.1), which provided a cause (hit a coral reef) and the result (salvaged timbers from the ship were used to build the first Spanish settlement in the Americas).

I was determined to find out to what extent each student comprehended this important content information, so I gave them a five-question quiz asking about the cause of this accident, the setting, the key players, the sequence of events, and the results. This method, the quiz, is a selected response assessment option because I chose the questions to which I wanted my class to respond. As introduced in Chapter 1, short quizzes, chapter tests, true/false tests, and fill-in-the blank tests are all forms of selected response. They are useful for assessing students' understanding of what has been taught—for literal-level recall of information, that is.

Unbeknownst to me, in the classroom next door, my colleague, Dorothy Syfert, also decided to assess her students' understanding of this same historical reading, but she elected to use a different method: she assigned her class the creation of a historical comic strip. Guess which assessment method was more popular, engaging, and enticing?

FIGURE 3.1
CHRISTMAS DAY, 1492

An Arawak chief approaches the Spanish fort to visit Columbus at the settlement of La Navidad.

Shortly before midnight on December 25, 1492, the *Santa María* ran aground on the northern coast of Hispaniola. Christopher Columbus saw his flagship perched on a coral reef and concluded, "I saw no chance of saving my own ship. . . ."

Columbus had been on his way to meet with an American chief who claimed to know a land where there was much gold. According to Columbus's records, when the chief heard of the disaster, "He wept and at once sent his people with many canoes to the ship. So we all began to unload together. . . . He saw to it that all our goods were located near the palace . . . [and] he set two armed men to guard these both day and night."

Columbus came to believe it was God's will that he lost the *Santa María* at that exact time and place. He also took it as a sign that he should found a colony there. So he chose thirty men, many of them volunteers, to build a settlement known as La Navidad—the Village of the Nativity.

Columbus left the settlers enough supplies to last for a year. He also gave them "seed for sowing, and the ship's boat, and a caulker, a carpenter, a gunner, and a cooper." Then Columbus began his journey back to Spain on January 4, 1493, aboard the *Niña.*

When Columbus returned to Hispaniola in the fall of the same year, he found La Navidad in ashes. The first Spanish settlement in the New World had ended in failure.

For Critical Thinking

1. What events led to the founding of La Navidad? Explain the significance of its name. What does starting and naming La Navidad suggest about the personality of Columbus?

2. Use a dictionary to find out what caulkers and coopers did. What important skills would they contribute toward starting a colony?

3. Scientists try to explain a given set of facts. Each explanation is called a *hypothesis* What factors could explain the failure of La Navidad? Can your explanation, or hypothesis, be proven right or wrong? Why or why not?

4. Use the map on page 54 to locate where the *Santa María* ran aground. Through research, find out what happened to the *Santa María*, the *Niña*, and the *Pinta.*

5. Provide several examples to show that knowledge of the past can be helpful in approaching situations today.

Source: Focus page, Christmas day, 1492, (1984), in *A proud nation* (p. 38), (Evanston, IL: McDougal, Littel, and Company). Reprinted here with permission of the publisher. © 1984 McDougal, Littel, and Company.

Visual Representations

The comic strip task is an example of performance assessment in the mode of visual representations. In this chapter we will describe a number of visual/graphic classroom performance tasks that help learners reveal their understanding of content information, that is, to Info Out (See Chapter 2). Graphic representations are primarily visual but may include written text. They come in many forms, such as:

- Comic strips, or other series of illustrations (e.g., storyboards)
- Graphic organizers (webs, clusters, maps)
- Large illustrations/displays with back-up text (posters, advertisements)
- Electronic presentations (slideshows, Hyper-Studio® stacks)

We're going to introduce four visual representation performance tasks. We will explain why we selected them, how we developed them, and how we scored them.

Performance Tasks: The Historical Comic Strip

The first of the four visual performance tasks we'll look at is the historical comic strip. This crowd-pleaser is an example of Stiggins' (1994) third assessment option, the performance task, because Dorothy expected her students to take learned content information and apply it in a meaningful task. That is, the comic strip task required her learners to put information to use, to apply their knowledge, to construct a personal response rather than merely regurgitate knowledge. In short, they had to *perform*.

So, naturally, I stole her idea for use with my class later in the year during our study of the Civil War. My students loved it too, even though it turned out to be more demanding than a test.

As much as this First Dare of the activity caused delight among the students, three serious design flaws emerged. First, the original directions called for five to six panels. (Note the content requirements at the top of Figure 3.2: A Performance Task: 1492 Encounter, "La Navidad.")

While this specification seemed reasonable at first, for some students, five to six panels was not sufficient space to reveal their comprehension of all the key events. This is not an atypical finding: many tasks reveal their design flaws when teachers examine actual student responses to the task.

Second, even though the task presented clear parameters to the students in the content requirements, many students did not realize that their comics would eventually be measured against these features. The scoring criteria were not explicit enough for all students to clearly understand how their comics would be evaluated. Again, this flaw is common to early task design.

Third, the extra credit component of the Share Stage (stated at the bottom of the performance task sheet [fig. 3.2]) made a huge difference in the performance of those students who opted for it. The decision to add extra panels and color highlights generally produced superior products. It ended up modifying the task for those students who opted for extra credit and, therefore, affected its validity —a common oversight.

Designing performance tasks for classroom assessment is a challenging process. Teachers typically find out that a great idea, like the comic strip task, will need "repairing."

Building a Better Task: Improving the Historical Comic Strip

Live and learn. Even with its flaws, the comic strip visual representation performance task had great potential to motivate student interest and effort, as well as to reliably assess student reading comprehension. We had to polish it to ensure that it became a true performance task and not just a great activity.

FIGURE 3.2
A PERFORMANCE TASK: 1492 ENCOUNTER "LA NAVIDAD"

Use with History Textbook: *A Proud Nation*, page 38.[1]
Designed by Dorothy Syfert, Monroe Middle School, Eugene, Oregon

Your Task: Create a 5-6 panel comic strip revealing your understanding of a key event during this historical era: the shipwreck of the Santa María, the causes, effects, and reactions.

***Content Requirements* that must be included:**

_____   5-6 panels
_____   At least 5 characters
      _____   your Taino Indian character
      _____   a family member
      _____   at least one other native
      _____   your sailor character
      _____   at least one other sailor
_____   Character names must be identified somewhere in the comic strip
_____   Storyline boxes
_____   Talking bubbles
_____   At least 1 thinking bubble
_____   The major events shown on page 38 of *A Proud Nation*.

***Process Requirements* that must be included:**

Prepare Stage
• Look through the comic strip examples provided by the teacher.
• Read page 38 in *A Proud Nation.*
• Decide on the characters to include.
• On the back of this sheet, write out a rough "outline" for your story. (Optional.)

First Dare Stage
• On a sheet of notebook paper, roughly sketch out what should go in each of your comic strip panels. Include words that will be written. (DO NOT SPEND A LONG TIME ON THIS PART.)
• Staple your rough sketch to this paper.

Repair Stage
• Go over the requirements to be sure you have included everything. Be sure you can check off each item.
• Check over spelling and mechanics.

Share Stage
• Get a large sheet of plain white paper and make your final comic strip.
• When you have finished, be sure to check for any silly errors.
Extra: *Additional panels* and/or *color* added to your comic strip.Display your comic strip on the bulletin board.

[1]Focus page, Christmas day, 1492, (1984), in *A proud nation* (p. 38), (Evanston, IL: McDougal, Littel, and Company).

Tasks differ from activities in two critical ways:

1. Tasks must clearly assess the targets being measured; that is, they must be valid.

2. Tasks must have clear scoring criteria, so that teachers can fairly, objectively, and, most important, consistently evaluate them; that is, tasks must have reliability.

After examining student samples of the original comic strip activity, we redesigned it to become a tighter performance task (see fig. 3.3, pp. 30–31).

Our feelings were not hurt; we understood the developmental nature of performance tasks. Tasks need to be fine-tuned, adjusted, "repaired" in order to tighten them up to reach the standards of reliability and validity. Performance tasks must have higher standards than activities because the stakes are higher: when tasks are used to measure student understanding and achievement, they must be fair and accurate indicators.

The historical comic strip now met our criteria in that it

1. *Involved some degree of student choice.* In the revised version, our students could determine the number of panels, the sequence of the panels, the amount of text versus graphics, and which historical figures and actions to portray.

2. *Required both the elaboration of core knowledge content and the use of key processes.* The comic strip task required students to elaborate on what they had learned from reading the textbook (content) and to use both reading comprehension and project construction (processes).

3. *Included an explicit scoring system shared with learners in advance.* Students received a task sheet, a self-repair checklist, and a new scoring device that combines a checklist with a rubric (the ChecBric) in advance. This example follows shortly.

4. *Offered an audience for the performance that is larger than the traditional audience, their teacher.* Stu-

dents were asked to communicate to 5th grade history students what happened to the Santa María in a more engaging and memorable manner than a 5th grade textbook.

5. *Was carefully crafted to measure what it purports to measure.* The task now more clearly assesses readers' comprehension of content information.

The revised comic strip task eliminated the earlier flaws. And with the improvements came the realization that in order for the students to perform well—that is, to reveal their understanding of the content at a high level of sophistication—they needed more time. So we expanded this from a mini-task of one class period plus homework to a midi-task of three class periods as follows:

Day 1: Students read the task directions, the assigned textbook section, and the ChecBric; and started preliminary sketches on 4" X 5" paper panels. (Working with individual panels made later revisions less punishing than working on one large sheet of paper.)

Day 2: Students continued panel production, completed a "Student Self-Scoring Checklist," and reread (repaired) the text as needed.

Day 3: Students reviewed the ChecBric; placed panels in the desired sequence; colored them; glued them onto a large sheet of 17" X 24" paper; added name, date, and class period; and affixed their self-scoring checklist and the ChecBric to the back of the completed comic strip.

We were encouraged by the results. Students performed at a higher level than with our first attempt. While not yet rigorous enough to be an airtight assessment tool for large-scale assessments, this revised comic strip task is now a fair and accurate device for classroom-based reading comprehension assessment. We feel confident that using it in our classrooms provides a clear and accurate indicator of each student's reading comprehension of nonfiction texts, in this case, history.

Our Procedure for Building Better Performance Tasks

You are probably wondering if we had a process in mind when we developed this comic strip task. When we first started developing tasks, we worked from the seat of our pants. As we got better at it, we formulated a step-by-step process for building better performance tasks that we sure could have used from the beginning. Our steps now include:

1. Be clear about your targets: the skills and knowledge students will demonstrate and the standards that they will be expected to meet.
2. Be familiar with the critical traits and key concepts of a strong performance.
3. Create and describe a context for the task that will make it more meaningful and engaging.
4. Write a short description of the task.
5. Rewrite the task in a clear and concise manner.
6. Assign the task to students.
7. Develop a step-by-step work plan.
8. Provide work samples from past years to show students what "good" looks like.
9. Provide instruction.
10. Score the task and then make necessary revisions for its use next time.

As we provide you with more example tasks, see if you can identify these steps in use. We will elaborate on them in the following chapters and in detail in Chapter 6.

Step 10 raises the next question we will pursue: How does a teacher score student performances?

Options for Scoring Systems

To ensure fairness and accuracy of scoring performance tasks, performers need clear criteria spelled out in advance. Just as Olympic gymnasts know very well in advance of the competition how they will be scored, students deserve to know in advance what "good looks like." Grant Wiggins (1995) refers to this as "demystifying the criteria for success." Classroom academic performers, just like world class athletes, ought to be privy to the scoring system in advance of the performance.

Several alternatives are available to teachers for scoring their students' work: rubrics, checklists, assessment lists, and scorecards, among others. Each has its own strengths in providing feedback to students and informing the teacher's instruction.

Rubrics

A rubric is simply a set of scoring guidelines for evaluating student work. Rubrics answer the questions:

- By what criteria should performance be judged?
- What does the range in the quality of performance look like?

Therefore, rubrics generally contain a scoring scale and a set of descriptors for each level of performance. They can be *holistic* (including one general descriptor for performance as a whole) or *analytic* (including multiple traits, sometimes called dimensions, with each trait being scored). They can be *generic*—used in scoring several tasks or *task specific*—crafted for a particular project or performance. The scaling mechanism can have any number of points but generally has four, five, or six. The scale can be *longitudinal* or *relative*. On a longitudinal scale, each point describes the development of skills and concepts over time from novice to expert. On a relative scale, each point represents the range of this performance from weak to strong. Figure 3.4 (pp. 32–33) provides an example of an analytical trait rubric used to score student work when deliberating on public issues. Its scale is designed to be more longitudinal than relative.

FIGURE 3.3
A PERFORMANCE TASK: 1864 HISTORICAL COMIC STRIP

Your **task** is to create a historical comic strip about "A Fiery Plot," page 434 of your supplemental textbook.

Audience and Purpose: The purpose of this comic strip is to explain to younger students, 5th graders, what happened in this little known historical event. Your job is to teach this event in a more interesting way than the textbook did, so that 5th graders will be inclined to *understand it* and to *remember it.*

Your comic strip should:

1. Reveal your **understanding** of the event
   - *Who* was involved?
   - *What* did they do?
   - *When* did this event occur?
   - *Where* did this event occur?
   - *Why* did they do it? *What* were their motivations?
   - *How* did it affect people?

2. Show the event in a clear and accurate **sequence**

You may have as many panels in your comic strip as you want, but the panels should show the events in the correct order, so that 5th graders won't get confused about what actually happened.

3. **Authentically** show what it was like during the Civil War Era

The characters' language and appearance and the scenery should all be realistic for the 1860s.

4. **Make it look like** an actual comic strip

Don't worry: Your drawing ability is NOT important in this task. This is a history class, not an art class, so what is important is how well you understood the event "A Fiery Plot," not how well you can draw.

Stick figures are OKAY. However, you should use *cartoonists' devices* to show what you know about the event:

- To show dialogue use

- To show thoughts use a thought bubble

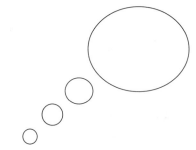

FIGURE 3.3
A PERFORMANCE TASK: 1864 HISTORICAL COMIC STRIP *(continued)*

- To show the narrator's words use a storyline box somewhere inside the panel

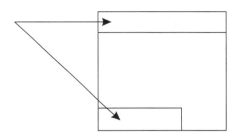

- To show characters' reactions, use simple facial expressions

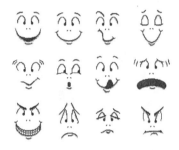

Historically, rubrics were red annotations used in church missals. These rubrics gave cues to priests and congregants on how to behave during worship. In the same way, teachers use them today to cue students on how to behave—how to successfully fulfill a performance task's requirements.

Checklists

A checklist identifies critical traits that must be present in the performance (like a rubric) and provides opportunities for students to indicate the presence of the traits by checking them off as completed or not completed. Unlike a rubric, the checklist does not offer a scoring scale nor descriptors for levels of proficiency.

Here is a sample checklist we used with students for a news conference activity:

__ 1. I have created a written draft of my presentation.

__ 2. I have practiced giving my presentation.

__ 3. When presenting, I speak fluently.

__ 4. I use eye contact and gestures to keep the audience interested.

__ 5. I have presented my presentation to a group of students in this class or another class.

__ 6. I have given my presentation to my parents.

__ 7. In my journal I have prepared a list of possible questions that I might be asked.

__ 8. I am prepared to answer these and other questions after my presentation.

FIGURE 3.4
SAMPLE RUBRIC FOR SCORING STUDENTS' ANALYSIS OF PUBLIC ISSUES

	Content	Issue Analysis	Action Proposal or Position
	This trait refers to the ability to select, understand, and use appropriate information (facts, concepts, theories, etc.) to guide and support issue deliberation.	This trait refers to the ability to use critical thinking to analyze the issue from multiple perspectives.	This trait refers to taking, supporting, and communicating a position and/or proposing relevant actions through the use of argument and persuasion.
6			
5	• The student presents a breadth and depth of relevant and accurate information and concepts applicable to the issue. This information focuses on substantive problems and themes related to the issue as opposed to facts and details only. • When applicable, the student demonstrates the relationship of particular democratic principles, including the rule of law, rights and responsibilities, liberty, justice, equality, due process, and civic participation to this issue.	• The student clearly identifies and succinctly states the central issue and its relationship to other issues. • The student analyzes the issue using several methods of inquiry from a broad range of disciplines including history, geography, economics, and political science. • The student identifies interested parties and presents their multiple perspectives on the issue. The student articulates and evaluates the reasoning, assumptions, and evidence supporting each perspective. • The student considers and clearly articulates broad public interests when deliberating on this issue.	• The student takes and communicates a position and/or proposes relevant actions. The proposal/position is creative, clear, coherent, and supported with unusually rich details. • The student explains the proposal or position and provides clear and convincing reasoning and evidence in support of it. • In a rigorous examination, the student identifies the consequences over time of taking this position or proposing this action.
4	• The student presents relevant and accurate information and concepts applicable to the issue. This information is based on fact as well as opinion. Data are drawn from a variety of sources, and connections are made between data collected from these various sources. • When applicable, the student demonstrates an understanding of democratic principles, including the rule of law, rights and responsibilities, liberty, justice, equality, due process, and civic participation.	• The student identifies the central issue and states it precisely. • The student analyzes the issue using various methods of inquiry from history, geography, economics, political science, and other relevant disciplines. • The student identifies interested parties and presents their multiple perspectives on the issue. • The student considers and states broad public interests when deliberating on this issue.	• The student takes and communicates a position and/or proposes relevant actions. The proposal/position is clear and well developed and has qualities that are distinctive or original. • The student explains the proposal or position and supports it with persuasive evidence. • In a thoughtful examination, the student identifies long-term consequences of taking this position or proposing this action.

FIGURE 3.4
SAMPLE RUBRIC FOR SCORING STUDENTS' ANALYSIS OF PUBLIC ISSUES (continued)

	Content	Issue Analysis	Action Proposal or Position
3	• The student presents relevant and accurate information (facts, rules, or details) applicable to the issue. This information is based on fact as well as opinion. • When applicable, the student demonstrates an understanding of democratic principles, including the rule of law, rights and responsibilities, liberty, justice, equality, due process, and civic participation.	• The student identifies the central issue but states it in general terms. • The student analyzes the issue using one or two methods of inquiry drawn from a limited number of disciplines. • The student identifies one or two interested parties and presents their perspectives on the issue. • The student considers and states local and regional public interests when deliberating on this issue.	• The student takes and communicates a position and/or proposes relevant actions. The proposal/position is clear and well developed. • The student explains the proposal or position and supports with some evidence. • The student identifies obvious long-term consequences of taking this position or proposing or proposing this action.
2	• The student presents some information applicable to the issue. The information is a combination of fact and opinion, is narrow in focus, and is from a limited number of sources. • When applicable, the student demonstrates an understanding of some democratic principles, including laws, rights and responsibilities, and civic participation.	• The student identifies the central issue but states it in very simplistic terms. • The student analyzes the issue using methods and reasoning provided by others. • The student presents at least two perspectives on the issue. • The student considers and states personal or localized interests when deliberating on this issue.	• The student takes a position and/or proposes actions that are simplistic and/or impractical. • The student explains and supports the position/action proposal with evidence that is simplistic and limited in scope. • The student identifies some short-term consequences of taking this position or proposing this action.
1	• The student presents limited, simplistic information about the issue. Information is based on personal knowledge and opinion or has been provided by others. • The student demonstrates little or no understanding of democratic principles, including rules, rights, and responsibilities.	• The student has trouble identifying the central issue and presents the issue statement in vague or ambiguous terms. • The student does not analyze the issue effectively or appropriately. • The student presents his or her perspective on the issue. • The student considers and states personal interests when deliberating on this issue.	• The student does not take a position or takes a position and/or proposes actions that are inappropriate or do not address the issue. • The student does not explain the proposal or position and does not support it with evidence. • The student does not show consideration of consequences.

This rubric was developed by Eugene Public Schools in collaboration with the Oregon Department of Education. It was originally titled *Deliberate on Public Issues* Rubric. It is used to score student work produced when deliberating on public issues. Used with the permission of Eugene School District 4J, Eugene, Oregon.

Assessment Lists

Assessment lists, like checklists, indicate to students what essential traits of excellence must be present in the performance—but they go further. Assessment lists also provide a weighted scoring value for each trait. The teacher determines the relative importance of the traits by assigning a point value, such as 10 points, 5 points, or 2 points. Many assessment lists attempt to have a total of all the traits equal 100 points.

Assessment lists also tend to provide students with the opportunity for self-assessment in a designated column, before receiving the teacher's evaluation of points earned in another column. (See fig. 3.5 [p. 36] for an example.)

Now let's look at two additional scoring mechanisms.

Scorecard Rubric

A *scorecard rubric* contains analytical traits and a scoring scale. In addition, the scorecard rubric adds a point system that provides an overall score. This overall score can then be converted into a percentage or letter grade. An example of a scorecard rubric is the Criteria and Scoring Guide from the Lane County Project Fair found in Chapter 6 (fig. 6.9, pp. 124–129).

ChecBric

A ChecBric is a combination of a checklist and a scoring rubric where the presence or absence of a particular trait is noted in one column followed by the assessment of that trait's quality in the other column. (Fig 3.8, p. 40, is an example of a ChecBric for a historical comic strip.) Students use the "Chec" column to self-assess, while teachers use the "Bric" column to indicate the level of the student's performance.

Scoring the Comic Strip Task

When we first designed the comic strip, the task sheet contained a checklist of scoring criteria. After using it to score student work, we found it had some weaknesses. For example, consider the work of two 8th grade reader-cartoonists, Peter and Toby.

Peter was thrilled at the opportunity to apply his considerable illustrating skill (see fig. 3.6, p. 38). On the other hand, Toby was concerned about his drawing ability (see fig. 3.7, p. 39) . Even though the directions clearly indicated that "drawing is not the targeted skill—reading comprehension is," he apparently felt at a disadvantage. So on his own time after school he created his comic strip using electronic clip art in the school's computer lab.

Imagine you are the teacher/assessor of these students. You assigned the reading and the comic strip assessment. Which student created the better comic strip; in other words, who performed better? Peter? Toby? Or was it a toss up—close to a tie?

Actually, the answer to this question must be postponed until a more fundamental question is answered. What are we looking for here? What exactly are we assessing? The answer is: reading comprehension. The task was designed to measure the degree of understanding of the history textbook's account of the 1492 sinking of the Santa María, its causes and aftermath.

So the assessment question is: Who revealed a higher level of reading comprehension? And, equally important: How do you justify your assessment?

To be fair, as the assessor you must read the history textbook passage (fig. 3.1, p. 25) in order to know what the students were expected to comprehend. We did and identified those elements of comprehension in the La Navidad Performance Task (fig. 3.2, p. 27).

Are you ready to make a fair determination now: Who performed better and why? After reading "Christmas Day, 1492" (p. 24), compare the comics to the criteria in Fig. 3.5. Most teachers agree that Peter's (fig. 3.6) is "better" because he incorporates more of the "content requirements" from the task sheet than did Toby. Toby certainly is to be congratulated on his skill with computer clip art and drawing, but his strip lacks critical information from the text, namely what caused the crash and what happened to the remains of the Santa María. These two pieces of information are very important to the textbook excerpt, and Toby did not reveal them in his strip.

The World's First ChecBric

While the content requirements from the original task sheet seemed to be a fair set of criteria to measure student performance, Dorothy and I decided to fine-tune the scoring system. We developed a two-columned scoring guide that highlighted the essential elements in two ways. First, in the left-hand column we built in a checklist for student self-assessment. We recognized that our students liked using a checklist to evaluate their work because it made it easy to see which traits must be present.

On the other hand, we recognized our own need for a scoring device that moves beyond the binary "yes or no" of a checklist. Therefore, we incorporated a set of multileveled descriptors that identified the *degree* to which students met each requirement. This allowed us, as teacher/assessors, to provide students with more feedback—informing them to what degree, or level, of proficiency they performed. So the right-hand column became a rubric. Thus, the merger of the best features of a checklist and a rubric became the world's first ChecBric (see fig. 3.8, p. 40).

To create the ChecBric, we needed to determine the essential traits we were targeting. We revisited the original content requirements of the task (see fig. 3.2, p. 27) to attempt to shake out reading content comprehension from the comic strip form—two very different traits. We then asked ourselves, Besides these two traits, or dimensions, what others would an outstanding historical comic strip have, regardless of the specific historical event? After discussion, we decided to add a third trait: "extends beyond the text," because our state's reading scoring guide now includes it. What do you think? Let us know. Our under-construction ChecBric eagerly awaits your input.

So to reveal the students' comprehension of an account of an historical event in a comic strip format, we deemed that they should

• Understand and interpret historical events in the passage
• Extend understanding beyond the text
• Control the form of cartooning for greatest visual impact

From Another Classroom: The Historical Comic Strip Goes to 5th Grade

The comic strip proved to be a popular Info Out form with students. We used it the following year to assess other key events in U.S. history.

We wondered whether this performance task would also work with younger students. The comic strip task idea attracted the interest of 5th grade teacher Susie Fuller at Arthur Elementary School in Sullivan, Illinois. Her class was also studying U.S. history, so she decided to use it to measure her students' comprehension of the same 1492 event.

Her goal was for her students to put their new knowledge to use by showing the historical characters' emotional responses to the burning of the Spanish settlement, La Navidad. An additional trait to assess was their ability to accurately sequence the events. She provided her 5th graders with a list of required items (traits) and told them they were free to show more.

She decided to improve Larry's 1492 comic strip by providing students with a Plan/Prepare worksheet divided into six panels to help them decide in advance what to include. Also, she modeled and had them practice drawing a talking bubble, a key cartoonist tool.

FIGURE 3.5
PERFORMANCE TASK ASSESSMENT LIST FOR A SCIENTIFIC DRAWING

| | | | ASSESSMENT POINTS | |
| | | Points Possible | Earned Assessment | |
	ELEMENT		Self	Teacher
1.	Appropriate and accurate details of structure are shown.			
2.	The drawings show an appropriate number of views of the objects so that all of it is represented in the drawings.			
3.	All drawings use the same scale, which is clearly shown. The scale is metric.			
4.	Appropriate and accurate details of color, pattern, texture, and/or other physical characteristics are shown.			
5.	If appropriate, the relationship of the object of attention to its surroundings is accurately shown.			
6.	If appropriate, the relationship(s) between the structure of the object of attention and its function is/are accurately shown.			
7.	Labels are used accurately.			
8.	An accompanying text accurately explains the science intended to be shown in the drawing.			
9.	Drawings are neat and presentable.			
10.	Drawings use the space of the paper well.			

Source: Educators in Connecticut's Pomperaug Regional School District 15. (1996). *A teacher's guide to performance-based learning and assessment* (p. 120). Alexandria, VA: ASCD.

Flashback: *Processing the Content with Info In*

Let's flashback in time to see what we did instructionally in the classroom before administering the comic strip performance assessment task. In order for students to have a fair chance at performing at a high level on this reading comprehension comic strip task, each student needed solid instruction in how to understand the content that would soon be assessed. Just as a coach offers guided practice to athletes in preparation for a big game, so must teacher-coaches help their students gain higher and higher degrees of proficiency in the targeted areas, in this case, reading to comprehend historical text.

We call this process Info In—how learners process new content information. As explained in Chapter 2, learners at all grade levels need instruction not only in content (knowledge) but also in process (know-how). Remember, it is not safe to assume, for example, that all learners in any given classroom are proficient in the various Info In processes: reading, listening, manipulating, and viewing. Too many students in our schools do not have a sufficient degree of skill in using these critical processes. So before attempting to assess their comprehension of the content, we must address their processing of that content.

In order for those 8th graders to be prepared for the 1492 comic strip performance task, we needed to coach them to use reading comprehension strategies. We structured our coaching on the reading comprehension process by teaching students the generic four-step process approach: *Prepare, First Dare, Repair, and Share* (explained in Chapter 2).

Let's explore this process further. Good readers are skilled at *preparing* to read. By this we don't mean merely the physical preparation of finding comfortable seating, limiting environmental distractions, or getting a favorite beverage to sip. We mean the more fundamental get-ready-to-read

strategies of

- Tapping prior knowledge on the topic you're about to read
  - Setting purposes for reading
  - Predicting what the author may tell you
  - Scanning the text to recognize the writing structure (organizational pattern) the author choose (e.g., novel, short story, poem, textbook chapter, professional article, etc.)

To teach middle graders the critical first strategy of tapping prior knowledge, we sometimes use the K-W-L activity (Ogle, 1986). This three-columned device, the forerunner of many other tapping-prior-knowledge activities, teaches student-readers to think about what they already **K**now about the topic to be read. This surfacing of prior knowledge recorded in column one greatly facilitates the acquisition of new information by synthesizing it with the already acquired information stored in the reader's memory. Different students naturally have different prior knowledge about 1492, Columbus, and America's indigenous peoples.

Likewise, the K-W-L also helps students apply the second Prepare strategy: setting a purpose for reading. Too many students, when asked why they are reading something, respond, "Because we have to!" It pays to teach them that other purposes for reading exist. Column two is where students jot down their questions about the 1492 topic: What I **W**ant to know. Students can better tackle the text because they now have a stronger purpose for reading: to find answers to their own questions.

Finally, the third column of the K-W-L is a place for readers to record their notes while reading. Answers to questions in column two belong in the "L" column: What I have **L**earned about the topic. Additionally, other information can be recorded here.

FIGURE 3.6
PETER'S HAND-DRAWN HISTORICAL COMIC STRIP

From Another Classroom: The K-W-L in a High School Health Class

Of course, the K-W-L is used at other grade levels with other subjects. Tenth grade science teacher Scott Akers—at Jackson High School in Massillon, Ohio—used it in a unit on basic life support techniques to assist student cooperative groups with their Info In on the topic of first aid (fig. 3.9, p. 42):

> The K-W-L lesson worked well in my classes because it provided students the opportunity to ask questions about the subject matter. The group interaction allowed those students who would not normally participate to give input in a much more comfortable environment.

As students fill in the three columns of the K-W-L, the teacher can prompt them to be aware of the essential traits of the upcoming performance task: in this case, a first aid comic strip. While not being overly prescriptive, the teacher can "forecast" the key traits to the students during the learning in order to assist their performance after the learning.

The K-W-L gave birth to another Info In activity: the Folded File Folder (FFF) described in Chapter 2. By using either the K-W-L or the FFF, teacher-coaches are instructing their students in successful reading comprehension *prepare* strategies. And it is the use of strategies such as these that helps readers maximize their understanding of assigned readings. Later, when asked to reveal their understanding of what they read—a comic strip task, a quiz, or any other assessment option—students will be better able to perform at a higher level if they are practiced performers.

FIGURE 3.7
TOBY'S ELECTRONIC HISTORICAL COMIC STRIP

FIGURE 3.7
TOBY'S ELECTRONIC HISTORICAL COMIC STRIP

FIGURE 3.8
CHECBRIC FOR ASSESSING A HISTORICAL COMIC STRIP

Name _____ Date _____

TRAIT ONE   Comprehension: Understands the historical passage ("Christmas Day, 1492" [fig. 3.1])

_____ Identifies the main ideas
_____ Identifies significant detail
_____ Has correct sequence of events
_____ Makes literal interpretations
_____ Makes inferred interpretations
_____ Gets overall meaning

6	exceptional
5	excellent
4	proficient
3	inadequate
2	limited
1	missing

TRAIT TWO   Extends Understanding: Goes beyond the passage

_____ Draws connections
_____ Sees relationships between
  __ selection and:
  __ other texts OR
  __ experiences OR
  __ issues OR
  __ events

6	exceptional
5	excellent
4	proficient
3	inadequate
2	limited
1	missing

TRAIT THREE   Communicates Ideas Visually: Effective comic strip

_____ Uses cartoonists' tools
_____ Is neat
_____ Presents ideas in a visually pleasing way
_____ Controls language conventions:
  __ Capitals
  __ Punctuation
  __ Spelling

6	exceptional
5	excellent
4	proficient
3	inadequate
2	limited
1	missing

STUDENT Comments: TEACHER Comments:

Graphic Organizers

We've looked at the historical comic strip, AKA the "science comic strip" or "literary comic strip." The second visual representation performance task we'll examine is the graphic organizer. As many teachers do, I (Larry) assigned my 6th grade language arts class to read a paperback novel. During our study of the theme of change as it relates to migration and immigration, we read Patricia Beatty's excellent novel *Lupita Mañana* (1981). In it, a 12-year old Mexican girl crosses the U.S. border with her older brother in search of work to help their fatherless family. Like many other teachers, I wanted to uncover the extent to which each student was comprehending the book. By the fourth chapter, readers had been introduced to quite a number of new characters, and I wanted to be sure my class understood who they were and their relationships to one another.

Instead of using a *selected response* chapter test or check quiz, as I had used to measure comprehension of the previous three chapters, I opted for a *constructed response* type of assessment device—the web.

The web is another type of visual representation. It goes by many different names: webs, clusters, maps: we choose to call them *graphic organizers*. Over the years, all of us have assigned our students to construct graphic organizers to share their understandings of content information because graphic organizers allow students to indicate not only their understanding of the content information but also the relationships within that content.

Examine Theresa's web of main character Lupita and her relationships with the other characters in the book (fig. 3.10, p. 43). She indicates: (1) the untimely death of Lupita's father with an "X" across Papa; and (2) her mother's need to establish new relationships with the money lender and a widow in the neighborhood, while maintaining her established relationships.

As a teacher assigning this task, consider the key traits of a powerful graphic organizer: Ask yourself, What would I as a teacher expect to see in a high-quality response?

I asked myself the same question, but I had help. At a middle school conference I had attended a presentation by 6th grade teacher Beth Larkins, who shared with her audience a "Performance Task Assessment List for an Idea Web/Organizer (fig. 3.11, p. 45)." She and her colleagues in Connecticut's Region 15 (Educators in Connecticut's Pomperaug Regional School District 15, 1996) have identified 10 elements.

An Assessment List—described earlier as a checklist with assigned point values for each trait—identifies the critical components (traits) that must be present in a strong performance. Using such a list, students may self-assess their efforts, for example, in one column—before their teacher does in a second column—and make any corrections, adjustments, or improvements as needed. Additionally, an Assessment List, sometimes called a "product guide," reveals to students the relative importance of each trait by providing them, in a third column the "possible points," the weight their teacher has assigned for each trait's value.

Taking a Step with a New Technology

While my students appreciated the opportunity to construct webs (far more than taking a test or a quiz, they told me), I decided to increase their motivation to perform at a high level by assigning a second graphic organizer—this one to be constructed in the school's computer lab.

As the novel *Lupita Mañana* unfolds, the author describes a number of problems faced by the two protagonists (Lupita and her older brother Salvador) and how they respond to each challenge with a solution. Because many of these characters' solutions lead, in turn, to new problems, the web seemed like a useful device to show plot development: the connection between problems and solu-

FIGURE 3.9
10TH GRADE TEAM'S K-W-L ON FIRST AID

Students: Brandon
Justin
Ryan
Rob
Gabe

The Reading Process .... Prepare Stage Strategies:
• Tap Prior Knowledge • Set a Purpose • Make Predictions

What I already **know** about
First Aid

—someone's dieing, leave
them alone if you don't
know what you're doing.
—activate EMS
—give rescue breaths
—choking give heimlick
—never move body farther
than you have to might
go into shock
—elevate wounded areas

What I **want** to find out about
First Aid

—how far can you move the body
—what to do if extreme bleeding occurs
—what to do about a broken bone
—what to do if someone's eye falls out
—what do you do about 3rd degree burns

What I **learned** about
First Aid

—cutoff circulation if severe cut
—dress a wound
—elevate bleeding wounds above the heart
—people who have 3rd degree burns call EMS
—support a broken bone
then put a cast on it

Adapted from The Reading Teacher, (1986), vol. 39, p. 564.
Note: To accurately show the students' work, we've left errors uncorrected.

tions in literature. So I assigned a second graphic organizer: An Electronic Web on the Problems and Solutions in the Novel.

I cannot take credit for the electronic version of this task. Justin, one of my 6th graders, got behind on his web assignment, so he finished it at home electronically on his computer using a simple draw program. (See fig. 3.12 on p. 46.)

Not only was Justin's web clear and easy to understand, but he told me that doing the web on his computer was "a heck of a lot more fun than doing homework." Good news for any teacher. When I asked him how long it took to construct an electronic web, he told me, "Not too long, about an hour."

I immediately recognized both the advantages and disadvantages of his electronic approach. First, the increased motivation and clearer presentation of the computer-generated web surely were of great value. But the hour it took Justin seemed too long to be realistic, considering how much more quickly kids can draw webs using paper and pencil.

Fortunately, a colleague offered me a brilliant solution. Vicky Ayers, our district's technology trainer, showed me a set of computer-generated graphic organizers constructed by special education high school history students using a software program called Inspiration®. She told me how easily this software had allowed them to make pleasing electronic graphic organizers she calls I-Maps (*Inspiration*-Maps). Another graphic organizer software program available is Sunburst's® Expression.

Electronic webs offer students a heightened graphic capability by providing them with hundreds of different shapes for web elements, automatic arrow-connectors between elements, swift and clean relocation of elements if needed, and, of course, the thrill of living color. After acquiring a

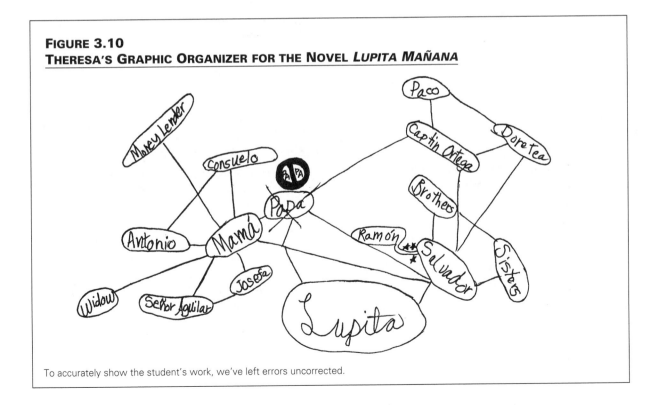

FIGURE 3.10
THERESA'S GRAPHIC ORGANIZER FOR THE NOVEL *LUPITA MAÑANA*

To accurately show the student's work, we've left errors uncorrected.

site license for my school's computer lab and installing the software, I assigned my 6th grade literature students an I-Map on the Problems and Solutions in the Novel (see fig. 3.13 on p. 47 for 6th grader Sameen's I-Map).

The electronic graphic organizer program created a more visually pleasing product as it also increased both student enjoyment and motivation for the task. But what about the more important consideration: students' comprehension of the problems and solutions in the novel they were reading? It's one thing to look good; it's quite another to reveal deep and clear understanding of the content information.

As classroom assessors, we must constantly ask ourselves:

• Does this task actually measure what it's intended to measure?

Putting it another way:

• Does this task really make students reveal to us what we are teaching?

In other words:

• Does this task clearly and accurately demonstrate student proficiency in the targeted outcome(s)?

Specifically:

• Is the construction of a graphic organizer a fair and thorough means for students to present to a teacher/assessor their comprehension of plot, that is, the problems and solutions faced by characters in literature?

And:

• If not, why not? What adjustments need to be made?

Or maybe:

• What is a better way to assess what we are teaching them?

If creating an electronic graphic organizer presents a problem for you (a lack of funds to purchase the software, limited accessibility to computers, or simply not enough time for this task), then you may wish to use an alternative task. Students can fill in a teacher-created graphic organizer. Figure 3.14 (p. 48) is an example of a generic template of a graphic organizer.

The World's Second ChecBric

Teachers must not only invent classroom-based tasks to measure our students' proficiency, but we must also assess the students' performance on those tasks. So along with the graphic organizer task came the need for a ChecBric.

Building on the Assessment List idea of my colleagues in Connecticut, I devised the world's second ChecBric based on three key traits of a successful graphic organizer, either traditionally made with paper and pencil or technology-assisted on a computer:

1. Information is accurate and complete to reveal content understanding.
2. Relationships among key information are clearly and accurately portrayed.
3. Visual appeal is apparent.

I kept the traits general so that I could use this performance task and its ChecBric with other reading assignments, not just with this particular novel. How nice it is to have generic tasks with accompanying scoring guides waiting patiently in one's file cabinet for repeated uses. (See fig. 3.15 pp. 49–50.)

As proud as I am of the ChecBric, I'm certain it can be improved. Try it out on Sameen's (fig. 3.13) computer-generated graphic organizers, realizing that your content knowledge of the novel *Lupita Mañana* probably is limited.

FIGURE 3.11
PERFORMANCE TASK ASSESSMENT LIST IDEA WEB/ORGANIZER

ELEMENT	ASSESSMENT POINTS		
	Points Possible	Earned Assessment Self	Teacher
1. Geometric figures are used. A large central figure is surrounded by smaller shapes.	_____	_____	_____
2. Geometric shapes are used throughout the web to convey relationships among elements in the web.	_____	_____	_____
3. The topic is listed in the central figure, and the main ideas connecting to the topic are placed in the qualifiers.	_____	_____	_____
4. An appropriate number of details support each main idea.	_____	_____	_____
5. The graphic information shows that the student has included enough information to indicate a thorough understanding of the concepts.	_____	_____	_____
6. The information is accurate.	_____	_____	_____
7. Space, shapes, textures, and colors provide information themselves and add to the overall effectiveness of the web.	_____	_____	_____
8. The web is creative: pictures, drawings, and other illustrations make it interesting.	_____	_____	_____
9. The web is neat, clear, and presentable.	_____	_____	_____
10. There are no mechanical mistakes (spelling, punctuation, grammar, word choice).	_____	_____	_____
TOTAL	_____	_____	_____

Flashback: Teaching How to Create Graphic Organizers

Just as musical directors train their musicians with thorough practice to ensure a flawless performance at show time, I assisted my students in preparing for their graphic organizers.

For a Prepare activity, I led my class through the creation of a problem/solution wall chart on butcher paper. Then I added a cooperative learning activity. Working in teams, the students reviewed a designated chapter of the novel to remember problems facing Lupita and her brother and their solutions. I then called upon each team to add problems and solutions from their review of the chapter to the class wall chart. This "reading-review-repair" activity served to remind everyone that good readers often *reread* to master content information in the book.

Next, I showed the class an Inspiration-Map that I had constructed on a different topic for another class. I demonstrated how the software allowed me to show both the key elements of the content and also the relationships among those elements by using selected shapes, colors, and arrows. During my demonstration, I used the "think-aloud" teaching technique: talking about the decisions to be made while performing the assignment. This revealing of the teacher's thoughts-in-action serves as a mental role model for kids who shortly will be completing the same assignment.

Finally, I retraced the steps for using the software. As my students watched, I directed them to make notes at each step, so that they would know how to do the steps independently in the computer lab the next day. In fact, their note sheet

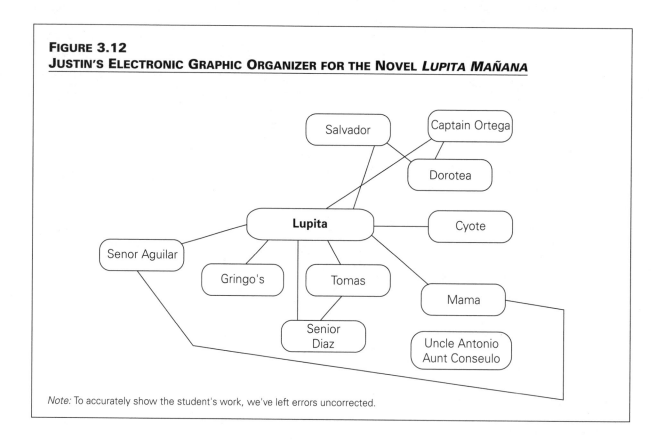

FIGURE 3.12
JUSTIN'S ELECTRONIC GRAPHIC ORGANIZER FOR THE NOVEL *LUPITA MAÑANA*

Note: To accurately show the student's work, we've left errors uncorrected.

would serve as a "ticket in the door" to the lab. Without it, a student could not begin the assignment. No ticket, no computer. The next day, two forgetful kids quickly tired of trying to argue with me and sat down to copy the steps from a friendly classmate. I was strict about this because I know from prior experiences the headache of trying to assist 30 or more kids in the computer lab—it's impossible to reach them all quickly. The required note taking increased their independence and proficiency with the new software.

Not only does this modeling/preview activity help the teacher with student management, but it also teaches the students how to use the required form of the task: if a graphic organizer is the selected mode/form, students deserve instruction in how to use that form effectively—whether it's in the traditional paper-and-pencil form or the technological computer software form.

From Another Classroom: Yours

Consider the potential of the graphic organizer task (both the traditional paper-and-pencil one or the new electronic version) and the comic strip task (historical, literary, scientific, and so on) for your own use. Take a moment to critique each:

- What do you like about it?
- With what content can you envision using it?
- What problems, pitfalls, or possible difficulties do you predict might arise?
- What adaptations, adjustments, or alterations might make it a better fit in your classroom?

An Adaptation: Adjustments for the One-Computer Classroom

One obvious limitation facing many teachers with the electronic graphic organizer is the avail-

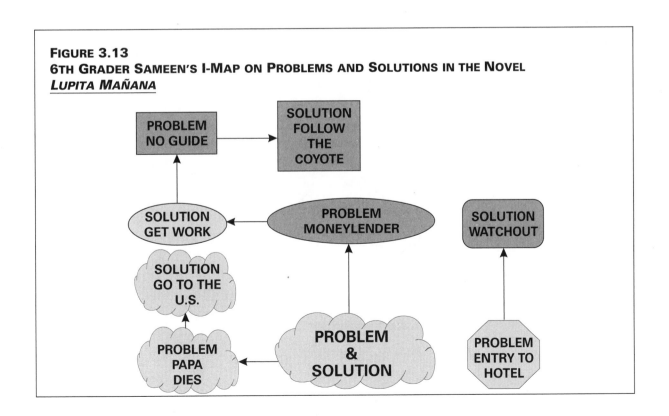

FIGURE 3.13
6TH GRADER SAMEEN'S I-MAP ON PROBLEMS AND SOLUTIONS IN THE NOVEL *LUPITA MAÑANA*

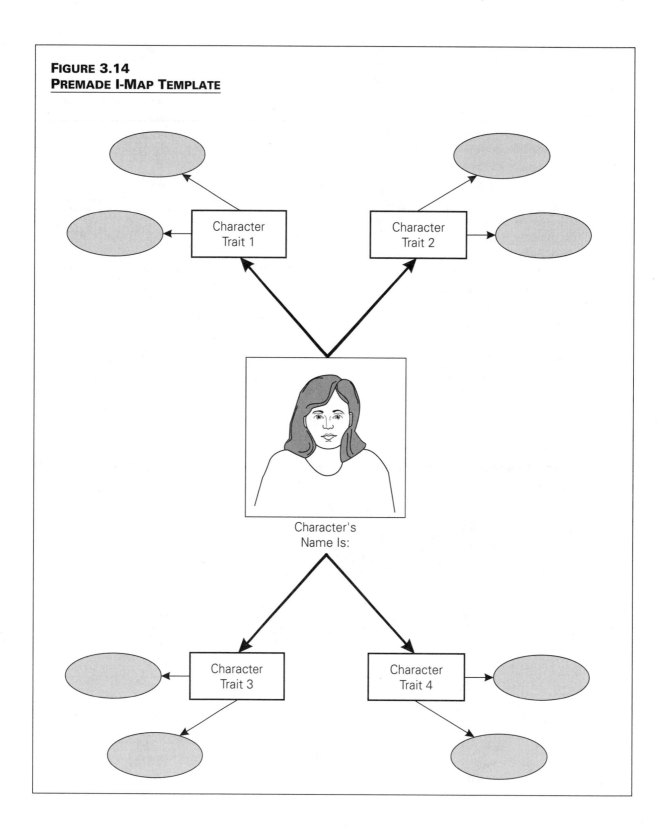

FIGURE 3.14
PREMADE I-MAP TEMPLATE

Character
Trait 1

Character
Trait 2

Character's
Name Is:

Character
Trait 3

Character
Trait 4

FIGURE 3.15
CHECBRIC FOR A GRAPHIC ORGANIZER
VERSION 2.1

TRAIT 1	Understands content information

____ presents important information ____ information is accurate ____ information is thorough enough to indicate understanding of content ____ level of detail is appropriate to age group	**6** *exceptional* degree of content understanding goes beyond grade-level expectations: • outstanding grasp of main idea and significant supporting details • presents interpretations, generalizations, and/or predictions based on specific and compelling evidence **5** *excellent* degree of content understanding represents high-quality grade-level work: • thorough and accurate grasp of main idea and significant supporting details • presents interpretations, generalizations, and/or predictions based on specific and solid evidence **4** *proficient* degree of content understanding fulfills grade-level standard: • indicates an understanding of main ideas and relevant specific supporting details • presents obvious interpretations, generalizations, and/or predictions based on adequate but not exhaustive evidence **3** *inadequate* degree of content understanding falls a bit short: • correctly identifies some main ideas; focuses on isolated details or misunderstandings or omits some significant details • attempts to present interpretations, generalizations, and/or predictions; fails to provide adequate support. **2** *limited* degree of content understanding falls below grade level: • shows a fragmented, inaccurate, or incomplete understanding; presents random, incomplete, or irrelevant evidence • fails to provide supported interpretations, generalizations, and/or predictions, or provides those that are not supportable **1** *missing* degree of content understanding completely misses the mark: • no attempt to complete task as assigned

TRAIT 2	Recognizes relationships within content information

____ shapes denote consistent level of detail ____ connector lines reveal relationships ____ colors are used consistently ____ central figure stands out	**6** *exceptional* degree of relationship recognition goes beyond grade-level expectations: • shows recognition of both obvious and subtle relationships, and draws insightful conclusions from them by labeling arrows/lines • level of detail is impressive throughout without resorting to padding **5** *excellent* degree of relationship recognition represents high-quality grade-level work: • shows recognition of both obvious and subtle relationships, and draws insightful conclusions from them by labeling arrows or lines • level of detail is impressive throughout without resorting to padding **4** *proficient* degree of relationship recognition fulfills grade-level standard: • recognizes significant relationships by drawing arrows of lines to connect items • level of detail adequately displays understanding of relationships **3** *inadequate* degree of relationship recognition falls a bit short: • shows recognition of some relationships, but fails to draw enough arrows or lines to connect items • level of detail is not sufficient throughout **2** *limited* degree of relationship recognition falls below grade level: • does not identify relationships or connects unrelated items • level of detail is way below grade level **1** *missing* degree of relationship recognition completely misses the mark: • no attempt to reveal relationships as assigned.

FIGURE 3.15
ChecBric for a Graphic Organizer *(continued)*
Version 2.1

TRAIT 3	Uses graphics effectively

_____ visually appealing layout

_____ neat, clear, presentable

_____ uses appropriate figures

_____ colors, shadings are eye-appealing

_____ central figure is larger with smaller figures around it

_____ correct mechanics for language

6 *exceptional* degree of use of graphics goes beyond grade-level expectations:
- professional look to it; very high-quality presentation
- color, shapes, sizes, and connecting lines or arrows are neatly and accurately placed
- text is pleasing to read
- no errors in language mechanics

5 *excellent* degree of use of graphics represents high-quality grade-level work:
- a high-quality presentation
- color, shapes, sizes, and connecting lines or arrows are neatly and accurately placed
- text is easy to read
- no errors in language mechanics/only a few that don't affect viewer

4 *proficient* degree of use of graphics fulfills grade-level standard:
- pleasing look to it; neat, clear, presentable
- color, shapes, sizes, and connecting lines or arrows work to unite the items
- text is easy to read
- errors in language mechanics, while obvious, don't detract much from overall impression

3 *inadequate* degree of use of graphics falls a bit short:
- may be neat enough, but not pleasing to look at
- color, shapes, sizes, and connecting lines or arrows don't always work to unite the items
- problems reading the text
- errors in language mechanics are obvious and begin to detract from overall impression

2 *limited* degree of use of graphics falls below grade level:
- presentation is marred; sloppiness interferes
- choice or lack of color hurts display; shapes, sizes, and connectors may be inconsistent
- text may be messy and difficult to read in places

1 *missing* degree of use of graphics completely misses the mark:
- no attempt to use graphics as assigned

Source: This assessment draws on the work of the Oregon Department of Education's Reading Scoring Guide, Connecticut Region 15's Performance Task Assessment List for Idea Web/Organizer; Center for Learning, Assessment, and School Structure's Visual Presentation criteria.

Teacher Comments:

_____
_____
_____

Student Self-Reflection on Task:

_____
_____
_____

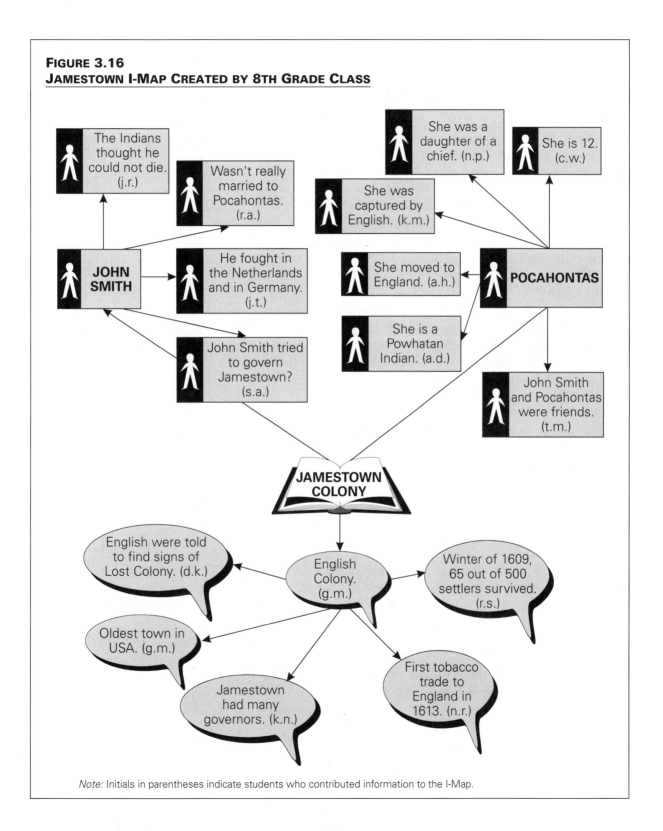

FIGURE 3.16
JAMESTOWN I-MAP CREATED BY 8TH GRADE CLASS

Note: Initials in parentheses indicate students who contributed information to the I-Map.

ability of computers. Not all of us have access to an up-to-date computer lab stocked with great software.

An alternative to taking a class of students to the computer lab to construct individual computer-generated graphic organizers is to have the class create a "collective web" on your classroom computer. For example, when my class of 8th graders was studying Colonial American history, they needed to gain content expertise on the Jamestown Colony and two key historical figures there, Pocahontas and Captain John Smith.

I used the Folded File Folder (FFF) activity (in Chapter 2) to tap their prior knowledge. I instructed my students to divide the FFF into three columns: Jamestown Colony, Pocahontas, and John Smith. The FFF provided the students with ample preparation for contributing to a collectively made class web on the classroom computer. To increase the likelihood of success, I deputized and trained one student as the "software consultant."

Throughout the week, I called individual students back to the computer to add one piece of information to the class's web with the assistance of the student consultant. Each contributing student chose which subtopic to add information to, based on what he or she had learned from the various sources. The student consultant demonstrated how to do this and asked students to type their initials to identify their contribution. At the end of the week, they printed a copy of their Jamestown I-Map and posted it on the bulletin board for all to see. (See fig. 3.16, p. 51.)

Two More Visual Representations: The Electronic Time Line and the Electronic Slide Show

We've discussed historical comic strips and graphic organizers. The last two we'll look at briefly are the electronic time line and the electronic slide show. Mary Kay McCann of West Chester, Pennsylvania, has shared with us a different performance task in the visual representation mode. Her class of 7th graders studied space flight, and to assess their understanding of the sequence of events, she designed the electronic time line performance task.

She gave each student a photocopied set of three resources on the history of space flight from its beginning to the space shuttle program. To facilitate their Info In reading, she instructed students to use highlighting pens to mark the key dates and to jot significant notes in the margins.

The midi performance task was to take the learned information and plot it along a timeline using the computer software program *Timeliner®* by Tom Snyder Productions, Inc. To ensure student success with this Info Out, she structured the task using the four-step process approach; she instructed her students in how to Prepare, First Dare, Repair, and Share their knowledge of the history of space flight by displaying completed time lines in the school's hallways. They enjoyed the process and gained proficiency in note taking and paraphrasing.

I have started having students use another visual representation task: the electronic slide show. Having grown tired over the years of hearing a collective groan from students when assigned another book report, I decided to spruce up this age-old performance task with computer-generated slide shows. I asked my students to create a series of "slides" on their computers with text and graphics that would inform other students about the book they had read. The individual slides then can be looped together to present an electronic slide show that can be viewed either on the computer's screen, or for larger audiences on the color TV monitor connected to the computer through a video adapter device.

Many software programs with the slide show capacity are available, from the sophisticated Microsoft's Power Point®, to more simplified programs for younger users; for example, ClarisWorks® or HyperStudio®. If you're a novice computer user, don't feel intimidated. These programs are all designed to guide you step by step through creating a slide show.

Just as with the electronic version of the graphic organizer, the computer-generated slide show performance task is very popular with students, who are motivated to produce high-quality work.

Snapshot of Chapter 3

In Chapter 2 we focused on how students use the key processes of reading, listening, viewing, and hands-on manipulating to take in core knowledge content. In this chapter we concentrated on how students show what they have learned/what they know through our first Info Out mode: *visual representations*. Visual representations are tasks that rely more on the visual factor than either written or spoken words. The four tasks we described are:

- Comic strips (historical)
- Graphic organizers (webs, clusters, maps)
- Electronic slide show book reports
- Electronic time lines

Visual representation tasks, like other tasks, need some revision to fine-tune them. We also shared with you the world's first ChecBric: a new scoring mechanism that combines the best features of a checklist and a rubric.

Here are some questions to reflect on:

• What activities using visual representations suggested here might you use in your classroom?
• Do you currently assess student progress before, during, and after instruction?
• What do you think of the ChecBric?

Classroom-based performance assessments increase the teacher's capacity to measure which students are learning what is being taught, and to what degree they're learning it. Visual representations contribute strongly to increasing teachers' confidence in our assessments. Using any of these tasks, we gain important insights into our students' learning.

And, as a bonus, kids love creating visual representations. Susie Fuller, 5th grade teacher, surely was pleased with the results:

> My students need variety in the way they are assessed. They got excited when I told them we wouldn't have a written test over the Taino/Columbus unit. When they found out about the historical comic strip task, I actually received applause!

Imagine that.

John Wetten Elem.
Gladstone, OR

Info Out: Assessing Students' Understanding Using the Written Mode

➤ An introduction to Info Out through the use of the writing process
➤ Analytical trait writing assessment

Larry's Happy Story

We had just completed an in-depth study of the historical relationships between the Spanish newcomers under the command of Christopher Columbus, and the Taino tribe, the Native Americans of the Caribbean. I congratulated my 8th graders on how well they had learned new information about this important historical content:

> You have succeeded at gaining new content expertise about the 1492 period—a subject that you initially thought would be boring and redundant because of your 5th grade study of the European explorers. I am proud of how much you've learned and how well you used key strategies to acquire that knowledge.

I continued by expressing hope that my next year's class would be as successful. I offered them an opportunity to assist me in making that happen: "Next fall, I'd really prefer to sit at my desk and read the daily newspaper instead of teaching.

How about if you take over and teach the new kids?"

This prospect got their undivided attention. "How might we do that?" they asked.

I suggested that they write a "technical training manual" with each student contributing a chapter to a class-authored "complete-how-to-do-it-guide" for the unit (see fig. 4.1).

I figured that by tapping into my students' expertise on how to succeed at the unit, I would accomplish three important objectives:

1. Find out what they had learned and remembered from the unit (Info In).

2. Teach them how to compose technical writing: a challenging, important, and often neglected, written mode (Info Out).

3. Motivate them to share this information by appealing to their natural desire to play the role of expert to younger students.

FIGURE 4.1
A PERFORMANCE TASK: WRITING THE 1492 UNIT TECHNICAL TRAINING MANUAL

Task: Write a chapter for our booklet on how to succeed in the 1492 Unit on Relationships.

Writing Mode: Expository (Technical)

Purpose: To help your teacher do a better job next year: Share your wisdom, knowledge, and experience with students who will be assigned the same unit activities as you were. Teach them how to succeed at producing high-quality work.

Procedure:

1. Select a chapter topic that you particularly enjoyed and that you were particularly successful at:
   - Chapter 1: Construction of Caribbean Island
   - Chapter 2: Construction of Taino character
   - Chapter 3: Construction of Spanish sailor face
   - Chapter 4: How to read historical fiction novels
   - Chapter 5: How to write an original historical fiction story

2. Review your working folder for work samples related to your topic.

3. Write a *First Da*re chapter with tips on how to do well, steps to follow, and advice on how to avoid problems. Save and print.

4. Meet with another student who has written a draft on the same chapter that you have. Co-edit each other's chapters by combining them into a single outstanding chapter. Save and print.

5. Conduct three rounds of *Repair:* Auto-edit your coauthored chapter, ask another student to read and *Repair*, and find a kindhearted adult to do the same. Remember to use different colored pencils for each round.

Assessment:

Your chapter will be scored on the following traits of excellence:
- **Accurate** description of the project, not incorrect information
- **Elaborate** information, plenty of detail
- Proper **sequence:** a clear order of how to do it
- **Format** easy to follow; correct paragraphs, punctuation, and spelling

Using Writing to "Show What You Know"

As teachers, we surely know the value of using the written mode to find out what our students have learned. Too often, however, we have used writing in the form of Stiggins'(1994) assessment type one, the *selected response* (paper-and-pencil tests/quizzes), and for older learners, its lengthier cousin, assessment type two, the *essay*. While using the mode of writing in these two ways is perfectly acceptable, Betty and I explored ways to move beyond the traditional use of the written mode to the more open-ended performance task assessment option.

In this chapter we present a variety of tasks using the written mode to assess students' acquisition of content knowledge. We will explore various forms of writing (letters, training manuals, reports, stories, magazines), share model "performance task sheets," and demonstrate how to score student writing.

Among the countless opportunities for revealing content understanding through written work, we will focus on our favorite performance tasks that can be administered before, during, and at the end of a unit or course.

We will illustrate how to design these written performance tasks, how they mesh with the teaching of key content, and how they are assessed. We will begin with *end-of-unit written tasks*. We'll look at four different types:

1. A technical training manual
2. A parent advisory brochure
3. A historical fiction story
4. A magazine or newspaper

Using Writing to Assess Students' Understanding After Instruction

Let's start with the technical training manual, an end-of-unit maxi-task and work backwards.

The 1492 Unit's Technical Training Manual

To *Prepare* for this written end-of-unit performance task, I asked my students to recall the various major activities that had been assigned during our in-depth study of 1492 historical relationships. Our list included the following:

• We studied the climate of the Caribbean Islands, including the flora and fauna. Students used construction paper to make mammals, insects, birds, plants, and physical features to add to a class-built island replica on a large bulletin board.

• We studied the lives of Taino Indians living on the Caribbean Islands and created a historically accurate Indian character to be a motivating entrée to the unit by providing that character's perspective.[1]

• We studied the lives of Spanish sailors aboard the Niña, Pinta, and Santa María and created a historically accurate sailor character for an alternative point of view.

• We read two historical fiction novels set in 1492, one from the Taino point of view, *Morning Girl* (Dorris, 1992) and one from a sailor's perspective, *Pedro's Journal* (Conrad, 1991).

• We created a historical comic strip about the sinking of the Santa María (described in Chapter 3).

---

[1]We call this approach "historical personalism." This unit uses the Scottish Storyline Method. For more information on this method, contact Storyline Design, 333 State St., number 246, Lake Oswego, OR 97034.

• We wrote an original historical fiction story set in 1492 starring our two historical characters.

After some discussion, we decided to exclude tips on the comic strip as a topic for the manual. We agreed to use the remaining five topics as chapters in our manual.

Each student then self-selected one of the five topics and wrote a First Dare (rough draft) of a chapter for the training manual. After reading some of their drafts, I realized that my students had no clue about how to produce high-quality technical writing. I needed to back up and teach technical writing. What do you think of the following list of critical traits that I generated? Good technical writing

• Has a clear sequence of steps without missing any key steps

• Has diagrams and illustrations to support the text (if necessary)

• Provides a strong statement of the manual's purpose

• Uses language that is simple and understandable to the reader

The next day I gave my students photocopied pages from the owner's manual to my VCR. We read the directions together and critiqued the effectiveness of the technical writing using the four traits. This sample provided them with examples of both good writing and poor writing. Next time I plan to provide a variety of sample technical manuals, ones for how to install a computer video game onto your TV, microwave a meal, or repair a broken bicycle chain. Examining several models helps students "anchor" the expectations more clearly.

Next, I assigned writers who had drafted the same topic to work together to synthesize the "best parts from each First Dare into a top-notch chapter using what you've learned about technical writing." Candace and Stephanie cowrote the 4th chapter (see fig. 4.2).

FIGURE 4.2
ADVICE FROM TWO 8TH GRADERS:
HOW TO READ HISTORICAL FICTION NOVELS

1. To prepare for reading, look on the back cover of the novel. There will be a little paragraph; read it because it should tell you about the novel. It will give you an idea of what the book will be about.

2. When you are given a limited amount of days to read this novel, make a plan of how many pages (or chapters) to read each day or night. The teacher should offer you a blank calendar page to help you stay on target. You shouldn't fall behind in your reading.

3. While reading a chapter, if you don't understand something, reread a sentence slowly. If you can't see the sentence, maybe the print is too small and you should consider a different book with larger print. (Bigger print won't take as long to read!!)

Bonus Tip: Of the two novels offered in this unit, *Morning Girl* is probably harder to follow than *Pedro's Journal* because it changes narrators in chapters. *Pedro* is written like a journal, in one point of view.

The Missing ChecBric

Due to circumstances beyond my control (bus duty that whole week), I had no time to produce an assessment scoring device. Naturally, I had wanted to provide the students with a ChecBric to guide their written performance. (I have to remember that it takes time to build high-quality classroom assessment tasks with an accurate scoring tool. "Next time I will make it better" has become my mantra, and I find myself chanting it repeatedly with devotional fervor.)

Next year *was* better. I tried the technical training manual again, this time with my 6th grade language arts class. I built in the time to create a ChecBric (see fig. 4.3), using some of the traits identified on page 57 to assess their "How to Succeed in 6th Grade" manuals written for next year's incoming class.

Possible Adaptations to the Technical Training Manual Task

Of course, other technical writing tasks abound in other classrooms: how to succeed at a unit on the Middle Ages, how to write an effective short story, how to conduct a successful science lab experiment, how to survive immigration to the United States (written by ESL students at a local community college to share with other newcomers), or how to successfully survive Ms. Abraham's Biology II class. The possibilities are endless.

The various technical training manual tasks described above stress procedural knowledge (how-to), but they also reveal content knowledge. While detailing how-to-do-something, students simultaneously express their understanding of the topic.

From Another Classroom: High Schoolers Produce the Parent Advisory Brochure

Another Info Out written performance task that can be used effectively with older students is the advisory brochure. Seniors in Linda Christensen's English class at Jefferson High School in Portland, Oregon, studied children's fairy tales. But instead of the typical literary analysis of characters, setting, and plot, the class evaluated these traditional stories from a social perspective: how do fairy tales portray females, minorities, and working people? The discoveries were eye-opening, to say the least. Imagine revisiting your childhood favorites but this time armed with a critical eye on the subtle (or not-so-subtle) effects they have on young readers' attitudes toward certain groups of people.

Linda took this social analysis further. Her students were to apply their analytical skills to contemporary fiction: Saturday morning cartoon shows. Their findings were as powerful as those relating to the fairy tales. So powerful, in fact, that the students were bound and determined to share their findings with an audience who would care. Some selected to write articles for women's magazines, the local newspaper, *Rethinking Schools* (a national teacher newspaper), and church bulletins. One group decided to produce and distribute a parent advisory brochure, which they titled "What's the Grade, Doc?" Here are two excerpts from it:

> *Duck Tales:* At first glance the precocious ducks are cute, but look closer and see that the whole show is based on money. All their adventures revolve around finding money. Uncle Scrooge and the gang teach children that money is the only important thing in life. **C-**

> *Teenage Mutant Ninja Turtles:* Pizza-eating Ninja Turtles. What's the point? There isn't any. The show is based on fighting the "bad guy," Shredder. Demonstrating no concern for the townspeople, they battle and fight, but never get hurt. This cartoon teaches a false sense of violence to kids: fight and you don't get hurt and solve problems through fists and swords instead of guns. **D** (Christensen, 1991)

FIGURE 4.3
CHECBRIC FOR A TECHNICAL TRAINING MANUAL

TRAIT 1	Provides clear and accurate explanation of steps

____ Statement of purpose is easily identified ____ All key steps are described ____ The order of steps is accurate ____ Each step is detailed enough for the reader ____ Extra, unneeded information is removed	**6** Exceptional presentation of how-to-do-it: guide exceeds grade-level expectations **5** Excellent presentation of how-to-do-it: guide reveals high-quality grade-level work **4** Proficient presentation of how-to-do-it: guide succeeds at clear explanation and shows grade-level work **3** Inadequate presentation of how-to-do-it: guide attempts to explain, but has weaknesses **2** Limited presentation of how-to-do-it: information is unclear/inaccurate, work is below grade level **1** Missing presentation of how-to-do-it; no attempt to complete task as assigned

TRAIT 2	Includes diagrams/illustrations to support the text

____ Visual tools are clearly drawn ____ Visual tools are labeled ____ Visual tools are appropriately placed in the text	**6** Exceptional use of visual support tools: professional quality that impresses the reader **5** Excellent use of visual support tools: high quality at grade level **4** Proficient use of visual support tools: diagrams/illustrations succeed at supporting your words **3** Inadequate use of visual support tools: attempt at visual support, but weaknesses hurt overall presentation **2** Limited use of visual support tools; work is messy, misplaced, or unlabeled; work is below grade level **1** Missing use of visual support tools: no attempt to include visuals as assigned

TRAIT 3	Uses language and conventions that help the reader

____ Vocabulary is precise
____ Vocabulary is appropriate for the readers
____ Conventions make information understandable
   ___ Spelling
   ___ Capitalization
   ___ Punctuation
   ___ Paragraphs
	6 Exceptional control of language and conventions: vocabulary and conventions go beyond grade-level expectations
	5 Excellent control of language and conventions: vocabulary and conventions represent high-quality grade-level work
	4 Proficient control of language and conventions: contains a few errors, but vocabulary and conventions fulfill grade-level standard
	3 Inadequate control of language and conventions: attempted vocabulary and conventions, but errors interrupt reading
	2 Limited control of language and conventions: too many vocabulary and convention errors cause confusion
	1 Missing control of language and conventions: no attempt to repair vocabulary and conventions errors as assigned

On the back of the pamphlet, students listed some tips for parents to guide them in wise cartoon selection.

From Another Classroom: Yours

Perhaps you've hatched an idea of your own for adapting either the technical training manual or an advisory brochure. Here are some questions to consider:

- In what topic or unit do your students have expertise (content knowledge)?
- In what procedure or process can your students share wisdom with next year's class (process knowledge)?
- What might the possible chapter titles/brochure sections be?
- Could you use or adapt the ChecBric (fig. 4.3) to assess the finished student work?

Another End-of-Unit Writing Task: The Historical Persuasive Letter

While studying the history of Jamestown Colony in 1607–1617, 8th graders in my (Larry's) U.S. history/language arts block class were expected to analyze the events from both the Powhatan Indian tribe's point of view and from the English colonists' perspectives. This historical analysis was further extended when I assigned a written critique of the fictionalized version of these events in the Disney movie *Pocahontas.* As you will recall, the kids had talked me into showing the movie as a culminating activity to our Colonial America unit (in Chapter 2).

I agreed because, as their teacher, I was determined to assess (1) their understanding of historical events (content) and (2) their ability to write persuasively (process). Specifically, I wanted these 13- and 14-year-olds to wrestle with the challenging notion that history is often open to interpretation. That is, the events of the past can be described, analyzed, and explained in various ways, and the reader of history must sort through

them to construct an understanding of what happened. In fact, this goal of recognizing differing points of view is a required learning standard in Oregon. Teachers are expected to teach, and students are expected to be able to

> Explain an event or issue from two or more points of view, and explain why perspectives among individuals and groups may vary.

Second, my state expects students to be able to write to communicate ideas:

> Use a variety of modes (e.g., narrative, imaginative, expository, *persuasive*) . . . to express ideas appropriate to audience and purpose. [emphasis ours] (Oregon Department of Education, 1997a).

By knowing what the standards are, I know what I am to teach. But *how* I teach is my choice and responsibility. And I also have some flexibility in the assessment measures I use in my classroom. So I selected a traditional 8th grade content topic, the study of Jamestown Colony, as the vehicle to *teach* to the standard relating to points of view. And I opted for a new, engaging performance task—the historical persuasive letter—as the vehicle for *assessing* my students' degree of proficiency at the standard.

Some of the students approved of the way Pocahontas, John Smith, and Jamestown were portrayed in the Disney movie, others were offended by the "Disneyfication" of history, and some had mixed reactions.

For example, Erin loved it, and in a letter she wrote to the Powhatan tribe's present chief, she disagreed with the objections to the movie he raised in an open letter to Disney published on his tribe's Internet website. Erin argued the difference between entertaining and informing:

> I am an 8th grader at Monroe Middle School in Eugene, Oregon. I'll get right to my point. I really wouldn't worry about the Disney movie *Pocahontas.* It's true that a lot of people don't like it because it's not true

fact, and the little kids only like it because it's a Disney animation. I don't really care. I happen to like the movie better than the true story of Pocahontas because they fall in love, and it's really romantic.

I think Disney makes the story more interesting. I also like the characters' personalities better in the movie.... I think most little kids don't care; they might learn when they get in school, or even if they don't, it's not going to affect their future. It's not going to affect the Native Americans' future either. I know all this may sound backwards, but it's just my opinion. My block class has been learning about it for the last three weeks and I feel I'm somewhat of an expert on it.

Her classmate Jessyca completely disagreed, and she strongly expressed her opinion of the movie to the producers at Disney Studios:

I would like to know what right you think you have to take a beautiful story, like the one of Pocahontas, and change it around just to make money for you? Did you ever stop to think about all the other people it affected? What about all the little kids that will grow up thinking that that is what really happened to Pocahontas? You claim that your movie is historical fiction, but I don't think you even know what that is. I question whether or not you even know the true story of Pocahontas. Well, in case you don't, I will tell you. I am a expert of sorts on the subject. I have read books about her and seen a documentary on her life.

First of all, as you probably know, Pocahontas was only 11 when she met John Smith, not in her 20s as you portrayed her. She did not even fall in love with John Smith, in fact she later married another man named John Rolfe. Ratclife was not even half as bad or greedy as you made him out to be. The fact of whether or not Pocahontas saved John from her own free will is still being debated by historians today. And the way that it only took her about one minute to learn English, well, I won't even get started on that. Even the way you physically portrayed her could be taken as a stereotype.

Finally, Jeff concluded his letter with a different piece of advice to Disney:

I just thought that I'd write and tell you how I felt about your movie. Oh, and not to worry about some of the other letters you might be getting about this.

Thanks for your time.

Showing Students How to "Proceed in Order to Succeed"

How did I motivate these middle graders to analyze history and to be able to dialogue with adults through persuasion? I provided them with three key items: a task sheet, a scoring instrument, and anchor papers.

As with any excellent performance task, a written task must give students explicit instructions on how to fulfill the task's requirements—so they can achieve the highest possible level of proficiency. So when I introduced 8th grade historians to the Pocahontas Persuasive Letter, they received a Performance Task Sheet delineating the key components of the task (see fig. 4.4).

The format of this task sheet replicated the development of tasks designed by educators in Connecticut's Pomperaug Regional School District. We like how this format clearly and succinctly guides students toward the targeted standard (Educators in Connecticut's Pomperaug Regional School District 15, 1996, p. 137). Just as athletes are instructed in how to play the game according to agreed-upon tactics, the task sheet serves as a "game plan" for the task.

Second, to maximize my students' performances, as a class we discussed the essential features of an outstanding historical persuasive letter. Students suggested the following "traits of excellence":

• Accurate spelling (I wasn't surprised because they typically identify the surface features of writing first, i.e., the mechanical conventions of grammar, spelling, punctuation, etc.).

FIGURE 4.4
A PERFORMANCE TASK: THE POCAHONTAS PERSUASIVE LETTER

Background: You will be studying early Colonial American history, including an in-depth study of Jamestown Colony from 1607–1617. You will read various accounts of this historical period, see videos, and read two "open letters" about the Disney movie *Pocahontas*.

Task: You will write a persuasive letter about the movie *Pocahontas,* arguing your opinion of it as it relates to the factual record of this historical event.

Audience: You will write your persuasive letter to one of the authors of the "open letters," either Mr. Roy Disney, Vice-Chairman of Disney Studios, or to Chief Roy Crazy Horse of the Powhatan Tribe.

Purpose: The goal of your letter is to convince your audience that your point of view is valuable and should be considered.

Procedure:

1. *Get the historical facts:* Create a storyboard of the documented events of the development of Jamestown Colony, including the actions of the key historical figures: Captain John Smith, Chief Powhatan, and his daughter Pocahontas. You will have multiple resources (a biography, textbook chapter, primary sources, documentary) to read and view to help you gather these historical facts.

2. *Analyze an historical fiction account:* You will both view the Disney movie *Pocahontas* and read the novelization of it. Create a second storyboard for the Disney version of this historical event.

3. *Compare and contrast your two storyboards:* To show the similarities and differences, create a Venn diagram.

4. *Analyze either the Disney or Powhatan "open letter" for its use of persuasive writing techniques.* Disney has removed its Pocahontas section from its web site. The Chief's letter is available at www.Powhatan.org. Click on "Pocahontas Myth" at left frame.

5. *Write your own persuasive letter to the audience of your choice.* In your letter be sure to
• Provide an accurate synopsis of the historical record of this event
• Express your opinion of the role of entertainment vs. historical accuracy in historical fiction
• Take a position (point of view) on the movie Pocahontas
• Back up your position with as many strong reasons as you can

Assessment: See the ChecBric (fig. 4.5).

• Argument with reasons (I was thrilled that they knew that persuasive writing requires supportive reasoning).

• Sufficient length (I convinced them to view this trait not as a specific word count or paragraph minimum but rather as a fully developed analysis).

• Accurate spelling, again (No comment from me on this duplicated suggestion).

After they brainstormed a criteria list, I refined it into an assessment tool: the world's third ChecBric (see fig. 4.5). As noted in Chapter 2, the ChecBric is a hybridized two-column scoring device. The left column is a checklist for students to self-assess their performance before submitting it; the right column is a rubric for the teacher-evaluator to judge their performance. Some teachers like to have students self-assess in the right column and then conference with them to arrive at the final score.

Note that the Historical Persuasive Letter's ChecBric has three traits. Betty always reminds me to select a maximum of three to four traits. More than four is too many for students to track and is too laborious for teachers to score. If scoring becomes a burden, teachers resent assigning the task in the first place.

As useful as the ChecBric is in helping students know how to "proceed in order to succeed," student anchor papers are even better. If possible, I collect a range of work samples—from strong to weak—for comparison. Then I remove the students' names and present them to the class for scoring of the selected traits. The first time I design a performance task, naturally I lack student samples, so on occasion I complete the task myself, with strong and weak characteristics. My students then judge it using the ChecBric. It's the actual written work that reveals "what good looks like."

Possible Pitfalls

Time for a reality check. As successful as the persuasive letter writing performance task has been, certain pitfalls can trap students.

The first is the lack of historical content. If students have not gained a sufficient degree of content expertise, they are prone to base their analysis on opinion rather than fact. For example, some students who wrote the Pocahontas letter based their critiques on personal taste instead of the assigned historical fact vs. fiction issue. Likewise, some students rely on emotions instead of supporting those emotional responses with historical facts. (See the first student sample letter on pages 60–61.)

Second, some students forget the historical facts presented during the unit, so their comparisons of fact to fiction are evasive. One solution is to assign note-taking devices during the Info In activities (reading, listening, viewing) so that students have a concrete list of facts to refer to during the writing task. Samples include the Folded File Folder, the K-W-L, and the Venn diagram (discussed in Chapter 2). Another solution is to periodically lead the class through a review of the unit's accumulating facts.

Finally, some young writers use sensationalized language in their persuasive letters. Rather than constructing solid analysis based on facts, they rely on dramatic statements—such as those seen on television talk shows or in advertisements. In these instances, I remind the students that good persuasive writing doesn't need to rely on this type of language.

Possible Adaptations to the Persuasive Letter Task

Persuasive writing is a powerful Info Out mode because the learner must move beyond

---

FIGURE 4.5
CHECBRIC FOR A HISTORICAL PERSUASIVE LETTER

TRAIT 1	Understands and interprets historical events

____ States key historical events ____ Identifies fact vs. fiction ____ Includes critical details ____ Specifies setting (time and place)	**6** Exceptional understanding/interpretation of event: analysis goes way beyond grade-level expectations **5** Excellent understanding/interpretation of event: analysis represents high-quality grade-level work **4** Proficient understanding/interpretation of event: analysis fulfills grade-level standard **3** Inadequate degree of understanding of this event: attempted analysis, but missing key pieces **2** Limited degree of understanding of this event: bare-bones analysis makes it below grade level **1** Missing degree of understanding of this event: no attempt to complete task as assigned

TRAIT 2	Develops a convincing argument

____ States point of view clearly ____ Offers full reasoning to support position ____ Uses a strong organizational strategy ____ Uses elaborative details ____ Is aware of audience	**6** Exceptional development of your point of view: persuasion goes way beyond grade-level expectations **5** Excellent development of your point of view: persuasion represents high-quality grade-level work **4** Proficient development of your point of view: persuasion fulfills grade-level standard **3** Inadequate development of your point of view: attempted persuasion, but missing key pieces **2** Limited development of your point of view: bare-bones persuasion makes it below grade level **1** Missing development of your point of view: no attempt to complete task as assigned Source of Trait 2: Southbury, Connecticut, Regional 15 School District, 203-758-8250

TRAIT 3	Controls conventions of writing

____ Correct grammar and usage contribute to clarity ____ Sound paragraphing reinforces organization ____ Correct spelling ____ Capitalization and punctuation guide reader ____ Little need for more editing to polish for publication	**6** Exceptional control of writing conventions: mechanics go way beyond grade-level expectations **5** Excellent control of writing conventions: mechanics represent high-quality grade-level work **4** Proficient control of writing conventions: some errors, but mechanics fulfill grade-level standard **3** Inadequate control of writing conventions: attempted mechanics, but errors interrupt reading **2** Limited control of writing conventions: too many mechanical errors cause confusion for reader **1** Missing control of writing conventions: no attempt to repair mechanical errors as assigned. Source: Analytical Trait Writing Scoring Guide, Oregon Department of Education, Salem, OR 97310

explaining/informing and move to arguing/convincing a reader. You can adapt this challenging writing task in various ways:

• Instead of analyzing a video, students can read a historical fiction novel and write an analysis of the facts vs. fiction in it.

• In writing persuasive letters, students can target a variety of audiences—for example, they can try to convince a character in the book to take a certain action or try to persuade the members of the Newbery Book Award Committee to vote for (or against) the novel.

• Instead of writing to a contemporary audience, like the producers of a movie or the author/publisher of a novel, students can write to historical figures, for example, Dear Monarchs, as my class did.

• And while the persuasive mode is a powerful challenge to young writers, the expository mode is also effective; students can explain/inform about a book, video, article, or play without taking a position on it.

Using Writing to Assess Students' Understanding During Instruction

The Historical Persuasive Letter

Not only did I assign my 8th graders the technical training manual as the end-of-the-1492-unit performance task, but I still needed to assess their understanding of the unit's content *during* learning. So, near the middle of the unit, I checked in with my students to see what understandings they were mentally constructing.

Rather than rely on a pencil-and-paper test or a written essay exam, I selected persuasive writing again as the Info Out mode. Just as with the Pocahontas Persuasive Letter, I guided students to reveal their understanding of historical content information by writing a persuasive letter. It

makes sense to us to offer our students multiple opportunities to write persuasive letters—to fine-tune their performance throughout the year.

And, as always, I considered ways to gain my students' interest and to motivate them to perform at the highest possible level. I accomplished this by reconsidering the traditional audience and purpose for writing. Instead of assigning them to write to me (teacher as the typical audience), I told them to write a letter to Columbus's bosses: King Ferdinand and Queen Isabella. This got their attention. They were excited about the task. Imagine: they would rather write a letter to two people who have been dead for nearly 500 years than to write to their dear teacher. I took no offense at this: kids crave a variety of audiences and purposes for writing.

The Performance Task Sheet instructed them to write the Spanish monarchs a historical persuasive letter as an eyewitness to the historical events of this time period. The aim of the persuasive writing mode, as noted on my students' worksheet was "to persuade, to convince, to argue effectively for your point of view." Their purpose? "To persuade the monarchs to agree with your point of view about Columbus's voyages."

The task sheet told them to address three key questions about the historical content in their persuasive letters:

1. To introduce your letter, which *one key word* best summarizes your point of view of what happened during this critical historical period?

- discovery
- visit
- arrival
- exchange
- intrusion
- invasion
- conquest
- genocide
- other _____

2. What actual *historical evidence* can you provide to support your point of view?

3. What *opposing point of view* can you predict would be presented to the king and queen by someone else, and how do you respond to it?

A Standard, All-Purpose Writing Rubric

Not only did the students receive a task sheet, but I also presented them with a scoring instrument. Wouldn't it be nice to have a scoring device delivered to your classroom, so you wouldn't have to design your own? Betty and I have such a tool, compliments of our Oregon State Department of Education (1997). It is a multi-trait rubric that analyzes student writing using a six-point scale. Traits include: (1) ideas and content, (2) organization, (3) voice, (4) sentence fluency, (5) word choice, (6) conventions, and (7) citation of sources. We have included the "ideas and content" trait in Figure 4.6 (p. 68). (Please see the **Appendix** for the complete Oregon Writing Scoring Guide: Middle School Student Version, pp. 150–156.)

Try it out. Use it to score the following sample, Roberto's "Dear Monarchs" letter, for trait one: ideas and content.

> My Dear King and Queen:
> I consider the Columbus story to be a discovery.
> It is true that the Tainos were there first, but it was Señor Columbus who united the worled (admittedly, he thought he was in Asia).
> There was an "arrival," but that was only part of the discovery. There was an "invasion and conquest," but these events have been kept mainly by word of mouth, and as history clearly states to us, when things are kept by word, tens become hundereds, hundereds become thousands, plagues become massekurs, and fights become wars.
> I am not accusing the Indians of lying, only of exaggerating to get a verry important point across.
> But 500 years of exaggerating can create (through fault of no one) mistakes or even fiction.

Of course, Roberto's score for trait one will be higher than his trait six score (conventions), and he needs specific feedback on the strengths and weaknesses of his writing. Over time, with repeated use of the rubric, students will internalize "what good writing looks like."

An important note: We do not expect teachers to religiously assess all student writing for all seven analytical traits. Due to obvious time limitations, teaching to, and assessing for, selected traits (two to four) is certainly a sane approach.

From Another Classroom: 3rd Graders Read Fairy Tales

Not only do Linda Christensen's 12th graders read fairy tales, but so do many 2nd, 3rd, and 4th graders. The study of fairy tales from around the world is a popular literature unit in many elementary classrooms, including Linda Barber's 3rd grade class at Guy Lee Elementary School in Springfield, Oregon.

During this unit on fairy tales, Linda wanted to check on her students' Info In processing. She knew that by selecting a motivating performance task, she would increase the accuracy of the assessment because her students would work to perform at their highest level. Rather than waiting until the end of the unit, she wanted to check in the middle of the unit on two targeted standards.

She chose a Dear Character letter in which a protagonist from a fairy tale the class had read writes a letter to a protagonist (or antagonist) from a different fairy tale. In the letters, students were expected to reveal their understanding of target one: the structure of fairy tales through retelling the main story elements: characters, setting, and plot.

The kids were given practice time prior to performance time (letter writing). Just as a director of a play would never expect a cast to perform on opening night without benefit of rehearsal, so too should we give our students opportunities to practice before show time. Early in the unit Linda modeled how to compare two fairy tales' structures using a two-columned worksheet:

Title		
Setting		
Protagonist and two characteristics	Name: 1. 2.	Name: 1. 2.
Antagonist and two characteristics	Name: 1. 2.	Name: 1. 2.
Problem		
Ending		

The second major target of the unit was the concept of literary point of view. To teach this critical standard, the class read a number of fairy tales from the *Point of View* series (Granowsky, 1993). These paperback books contain two opposing versions of the same fairy tale narrated by a different character; for example, Cinderella tells her story followed by a stepsister's version. Naturally, the two versions differ dramatically and humorously, so the students quickly and easily understood how a story can be told from differing points of view.

Another clever book that teaches an alternative perspective to a fairy tale is Jon Scieszka's *The True Story of the Three Little Pigs*, narrated by A. Wolfe. (Scieszka, 1989). In a very funny rendition of the classic story, the wolf puts an entirely different spin to it. For example, he swears that all the "huffing and puffing" was due to an unfortunate head cold, and that the trouble with the pigs ("those little porkers") was caused by their lack of neighborly courtesy.

Next, Linda instructed her 3rd graders to select a favorite protagonist (e.g., Papa Bear or Goldilocks) and write a Dear Character letter from that perspective to another protagonist/antagonist from a different fairy tale. To give her students the best possible chance for performing well, Linda provided them with two items: (1) a sample letter (written by her) to critique and (2) a scoring rubric with two traits drawn from the Oregon Analytical Trait Writing Scoring Guide. Here is Linda's sample letter:

Dear Goldi,

Guess what! I made a bad mistake last week. Do you remember that my grandma was sick? Well, mom sent me to her house with a basket of bread, cheese, and wine to make her feel better. She told me not to talk to anyone and to go straight there, but here's where I blew it.

While I was walking through the woods I met a very nice (I thought) wolf who I stopped to chat with. I told him about Grams, and he told me where I could get some very nice flowers. I know mom said go straight there, but I thought some flowers would make Grams feel better, so I took a bit of a detour to pick some for her. I thought I was doing a good thing.

—Little Red Riding Hood

Figure 4.7 (p. 69) shows a rubric for scoring the Dear Character Letter.

After reading his teacher's sample letter, young Jacob opted to be Jack (of Beanstalk fame) and write to a famous antagonist, the Big Bad Wolf (co-star of "Little Red Riding Hood"). Notice that he circles spelling uncertainties in his First Dare for correcting later in the Repair stage (fig. 4.8, p. 70).

Possible Adaptations to the Dear Character Letter

Older students could write the Dear Character letter from the point of view of a minor character to the fairy tale's author, expressing reasons to reconsider the traditional plot to increase the minor character's role. Both point of view and story elements would still be the targets.

FIGURE 4.6: OREGON WRITING SCORING GUIDE

Ideas and Content Trait: Communicating Knowledge of the Topic, Including Relevant Examples, Facts, Anecdotes, and Details
Middle School Student Version

6
The writing is exceptionally clear, focused, and interesting. It holds the reader's attention. Main ideas stand out and are developed by strong support and rich details that fit the audience and purpose. The writing has
- A clear focus and control
- Main idea(s) that stand out
- Details that are on topic and carefully selected; when needed, use of resources provides strong, accurate, believable support
- An appropriate amount of detail (not too much or too little) to support an in-depth explanation or exploration of the topic; the writing makes connections and shared insights
- Main ideas and selected details that fit the purpose and hold the reader's attention from beginning to end

5
The writing is clear, focused, and interesting. It holds the reader's attention. Main ideas stand out and are developed by supporting details that fit the audience and purpose. The writing has
- A clear focus and control
- Main idea(s) that stand out
- Details that are on topic and carefully selected; when needed, use of resources provides strong, accurate, believable support
- An appropriate amount of detail (not too much or too little) to support an in-depth explanation or exploration of the topic; the writing makes connections and shared insights
- Main ideas and selected details that fit the purpose and hold the reader's attention from beginning to end

4
The writing is clear and focused. The reader can easily understand the main ideas. Support is present, but may be too limited or somewhat general. The writing has
- A clear purpose
- Clear main ideas
- Details that are on topic, but may be too general or limited; when needed, resources are used to provide accurate support
- Details that may sometimes be too many or too few for a thorough explanation or exploration of the topic; some connections and insights may be present
- Main ideas and selected details that fit the purpose and hold the reader's attention most of the time from beginning to end

3
The writing has main idea(s), but they may be too broad or simplistic. Supporting detail is often too limited, overly general, or sometimes off the topic. The writing has
- A purpose that is easy to find
- Main idea(s) that are easy to find but overly obvious or predictable; main points or conclusions repeat ideas often heard
- Support of main ideas, but there aren't enough supporting details, or they are too general, predictable, or somewhat off topic
- Details that may not be based on reliable resources; may be based on clichés, stereotypes, or sources of information that are biased, uninformed, or unreliable

2
The writing has main idea(s), but they are undeveloped, and the purpose is somewhat unclear. The writing has
- An unclear purpose that requires the reader to guess the main ideas
- Minimal development, lacking details
- Details, when included, are not well connected to the main ideas and clutter the paper
- Details that are frequently repeated

1
The writing lacks main idea(s) or purpose. The writing has
- Ideas that are very limited or simply unclear
- Few or no attempts to develop ideas; the paper is too short to demonstrate the development of an idea

Source: Office of Assessment and Evaluation • Oregon Department of Education • July 8, 1996

Of course, fairy tales are not the only genre of literature that lend themselves to character letters. Teachers routinely find opportunities to assess their students' understandings of literature through the mode of writing. For example, they can ask students to write letters to a character in which they express approval or disapproval of the character's actions, offer advice on changing an attitude, or reveal some key information that the character doesn't yet know.

Older students could be expected to go beyond character and plot description to a deeper analysis of the folk tale's theme/moral, or to a comparison of the tale to another piece of fiction. The scoring rubric would be altered accordingly.

The Historical Fiction Story

Many teachers employ narrative story writing in addition to letter writing to assess students' understandings of new content. Beginning in the primary grades, students can write stories based on Info In content knowledge. Stories about whales and dinosaurs, about Native American legends and Greek myths, about tornadoes and life cycles, all are possible assignments.

In the above examples, the narrative mode is actually merged with the expository mode, so that students are explaining and informing (expository) through a story format (narrative). Even older students can benefit from this merger. Read one 8th grader's combined expository and narrative piece about 1492:

> Oh, it was not a pleasant journey! I was 34 and had lived in Spain. I was an able-seaman and got paid $7 a month to sail on the Santa María, while the captain, Señor Columbus, got paid zillions.
> We ate hard biscuits and dried peas and salted meat for two meals a day. We had to eat with hands out of one wooden bowl between us all . . .

Teachers will recognize this type of writing as first-person historical fiction. The student shares her content understanding (of life aboard Columbus's ship in 1492) by way of story writing. She weaves the true historical facts she learned into an invented account of a fictitious character. James Michener himself would have been proud.

Now, let's consider using writing to assess very young students: Betty's 1st and 2nd graders during a health unit.

FIGURE 4.7
DEAR CHARACTER LETTER RUBRIC

	Trait One: Content		Trait Two: Conventions	
5=	I wrote about the story completely describing the characters, setting, and plot.	5=	My final copy shows that I made corrections in my spelling and punctuation.	
3=	I shared the main idea of the story, but I missed some key parts.	3=	My final copy shows that I corrected most of the spelling and punctuation.	
1=	I had trouble sharing the basic idea of the story.	1=	My final copy shows that I didn't correct my spelling and punctuation errors.	
Score		Score		

FIGURE 4.8
A 3RD GRADER'S DEAR CHARACTER LETTER

the Jack   10-14-96

Dear Big bad Wolf,
I'm Jack. I have stolen from the rich and got the gold
eggs including the harp and the gooberry et first started
when I bought this seed. They weren't just seeds. They
were magic seed but mom threw them out of
window. At night they grew higher and higher to the
clouds. Then I climbed up the bean stalk. I saw a
castle and a big giant's wife. I went into the
castle. I chopped the beenstalk and the giant fell
down and me and my mom lived happily ever after, and
then we were rich because we got the money from the
giant.

your friends,
jacob

Assessing Primary Graders' Health Knowledge

During a unit on germ transmission, "How to Catch a Cold," my (Betty's) 1st and 2nd graders became Disease Detectives and conducted controlled experiments to Info In. To assess their understanding of the unit's important concepts, I chose the Info Out mode of writing: the students were to write humorous pop-up books. The next year I changed the assignment: my new class was to write informational articles about germs and

colds for our classroom newspaper. In expository writing, I told the kids, the writer explains or informs the audience about a topic.

To guide them to success on this performance task, I referred them back to the key questions we had addressed in the unit:

1. What is your hypothesis about the relationship of germs to catching a cold?

2. What experiments did you conduct?

3. What variables did you consider?

4. What are the results of your experiments?

And I added a fifth question:

5. What advice can you share with a reader?

Their assignment was to write an article with information containing answers to the above key questions. I reminded them that the best articles would not only answer the questions for a reader (content), but they would also meet the standards of good writing (process). To score the work, we selected three traits from the Oregon Analytical Trait Writing Scoring Guide (ideas/content, organization, and conventions). See Figure 4.9.

Larry's Middle Schoolers Write Articles about History

During a unit on the Revolutionary War, my 8th grade block class spent three class periods learning about the 1770 Boston Massacre and its effect on the coming American Revolution. To assess their in-progress understandings of this important historical content information, I selected the Info Out mode of writing.

Just as Betty used news article writing, I, too, assigned my class an expository paper in the form of a news article about the event. My students

---

FIGURE 4.9
PRIMARY NEWS ARTICLE CHECBRIC

Trait	Score
1. I provided the reader with a lot of information. _____ My hypothesis is stated. _____ My experiment is described. _____ I identified the variables. _____ The results of my experiment are clear. _____ I give advice to the reader.	1 2 3 4 5 6 Comments:
2. My writing is organized. _____ I have a catchy beginning. _____ I have a "meaty" middle. _____ I have a clear ending.	1 2 3 4 5 6 Comments:
3. I checked my work and corrected it. _____ I corrected all spelling errors. _____ I fixed all punctuation mistakes. _____ I wrote a neat final copy.	1 2 3 4 5 6 Comments:

A score of **6** means that my work is really great.
A score of **5** means that my work is strong.
A score of **4** means that my work is O.K. and I am getting better all the time.
A score of **3** means that my work is weak but getting better.
A score of **2** means that my work is like that of a beginner.
A score of **1** means that I did not do this.

were expected to address the following key questions about this historical event:

- Who/what do you think caused the Boston Massacre?
- What were the effects of this event?
- What evidence exists to support your opinion?
- What is a different point of view about the cause(s)?

Ryan wrote:

> *The Boston News*
> Boston, MA—It all started one night when some kids were throwing snowballs. After that, the people of the great city of Boston started ganging up on the British soldiers. Then someone from Boston had a major stupid attack and started firing at them. We have reports of only five people being killed, but we will keep you posted.

To assess Ryan's content understanding, I first needed to determine what "good looks like," that is, what key traits does outstanding historical writing have? I did have the above key questions but, unfortunately, I hadn't fleshed out a scoring device before assigning the task (back in 1993). I assume I'm not the only teacher to assign a great performance task, collect the students' work, and face grading them without a clue!

Your Turn: How Would You Score a News Article?

If you assigned your students to explain to or inform a reader about a topic they had just studied (e.g., germs causing colds or the Boston Massacre) in the form of a news article, what would you expect them to do? What essential traits, or characteristics, should their writing demonstrate?

When asked this same question, teachers in workshops we have conducted around the country generated the following list:

- Accurate content information
- Proper sequence of events

- An engaging writing style
- Clear explanation of the causes and effects
- Evidence to support one's point of view
- Proper mechanics (spelling, capitalization, punctuation)

To prevent overload for students writing this assignment (and, later, for teachers assessing their writing), it would be wise to pare down the brainstormed criteria list to two, three, or, at most, four traits for which the kids would be responsible. Can you adapt Betty's ChecBric (see fig. 4.9, p. 71) for writing a "How to Catch a Cold" news article to your classroom?

Help Is on the Way

Consider the rubric designed by the Oregon Department of Education to score older students' writing in the expository mode. Use it to score Ryan's Boston Massacre article. How well did he perform? (See fig. 4.10.)

Using Reflective Writing Tasks

Reflective writing involves thinking about one's learning, both the content and process. Many teachers use "reflective journals" to teach students how to keep track of their learning. Successful forms of journal writing include a literature journal, a writer's diary, and a math log. Students record their thoughts about the literature they're reading, about struggles and successes with a writing assignment, or how they attack math problems.

Tim Whitley, a science teacher at Sheldon High School in Eugene, Oregon, uses a reflective log writing performance task with his 9th and 10th grade biology students, entitled My Biology Journal. To assess his students' understanding of ecosystems, Tim required every student to record thoughts, ideas, perceptions, illustrations, and/or facts in a spiral-bound mini-log. Throughout the unit, he reminded his students to make entries in

FIGURE 4.10
OREGON'S EXPOSITORY MODE SCORING GUIDE

DEFINITION: Expository writing gives information, explains something, clarifies, or defines. The writing teaches, reveals, informs, or amplifies the reader's understanding through a carefully crafted mix of key points and critical support.

5: **The paper consistently presents information in a way that expands the reader's knowledge or enhances the reader's understanding. The result is clear, comprehensible, and complete.**
- Ideas are unambiguous and fully explained.
- The paper makes a point that the reader can readily grasp.
- Fact, examples, or explanations provide strong support.
- The reader has a sense of learning something or understanding an issue/topic better.
- The writer seems to be working from a strong base of information, and can select what will help the reader most.
- The writer shows a concern for the reader, and consistently presents information in a way that contributes to the reader's understanding.

3: **The paper presents some important information, but the reader feels about halfway home in terms of understanding the point the writer is trying to make. The result is a mix of helpful information, together with some fuzzy or incomplete points.**
- Ideas are reasonably clear, but the reader needs to make some inferences.
- The writer makes a general point, or points, but hasn't narrowed or fine-tuned the topic quite enough yet.
- Facts, examples, or explanations provide marginally adequate (but not strong) support.
- Some parts of the paper seem repetitive or predictable.
- The writer seems to have *just* enough information to write about this topic, but not enough to anticipate and address all the reader's questions.
- The writer seems aware of the reader, but often tends to explain what's already obvious, or to make assumptions about the reader's knowledge that aren't warranted.
- The writer attempts to explain or inform, but the power of the paper to enhance the reader's understanding is somewhat limited.

1: **The paper is very limited in its capacity to inform or enlighten the reader. The writing is very unclear, incomplete, or both.**
- Ideas are extremely limited or hard to understand, even if the reader tries to draw inferences based on what is there.
- The paper cannot seem to get beyond lists or generalizations; it is more puzzling or confusing than enlightening.
- The writer does not seem to have enough information to write about this topic. Support is very weak or nonexistent.
- The reader has a difficult time gleaning any knowledge, insight, or understanding from the text.

**FIGURE 4.11
A 9TH GRADER'S REFLECTIVE
BIOLOGY LOG ENTRY**

LIFE'S SECRET

*A quick glance at nature,
       and life stands still.
But peeking closer,
       life reveals . . . ,*

*An endless cycle,
A busy chain
Mysterious wonders,
An intricate game.*

*The rules are a secret,
hidden behind an invisable [sic] muzzle
for who could ever decode,
life's magnificent puzzle.*

—Angela

---

whatever form(s) worked for them. Angela wrote a poem about life cycles (fig. 4.11).

Nathan (Larry's former student!) used annotated sketches to "show what he knows" about producers, consumers, and decomposers in nature (fig. 4.12).

To assess their understanding, the teacher responded to the students' recorded observations by writing comments, questions, and or suggestions on yellow Post-it notes and attaching them throughout the Biology Journals. This method seems very appropriate to us. Assessing students' reflective writing differs from assessing the other writing modes because the purpose and audience are different: to be personally thoughtful about the content being studied or about the learning process being employed. The audience, of course, is oneself. Therefore, teacher assessment can be gently probing and supportive rather than coldly objective as with a rubric or ChecBric.

Historical Reflective Writing

Of course, the more objective approach is valid, too. Cathy Bechen, a teacher from Shasta Middle School in Oregon's School District 52, assigned her 8th graders to keep a journal as a member of Lewis and Clark's historic expedition across the West to the Pacific Ocean. The content knowledge she was assessing is different from Tim Whitley's biology content, but the Info Out mode is the same: reflective writing.

Cathy set up the writing task by distributing a task assignment sheet with four steps for each team of student adventurers to follow. After making sure everyone understood the instructions, she gave each student a Lewis and Clark Simulation Task Sheet, which split the task into three subtasks: a chart, a map, and the journal (see fig. 4.13).

Notice that the three subtasks are weighted in importance—the journal being the most important Info Out component, so it was valued at 50 points. Here is one journal entry written by teammates Angela, Garrett, Darcy, Danielle, and Joe. Read to see how they revealed their understanding of this historical event by writing reflectively about it as if they were experiencing it firsthand through the eyes of a historical character:

May 16, 1804

Dear Journal,
    Today we encountered a Shoshone Indian woman along the way. We decided to bring her with us, for an interpreter.
    Many of the our men are sick with dysentery and boils. I believe that the dysentery came from drinking the river water, which was very rich in sediment.
    The boils are the men working too hard and sweating which resulted in extreme exhaustion.
    Earlier today I went down to the river and discovered a fish that I've never seen before. . . .

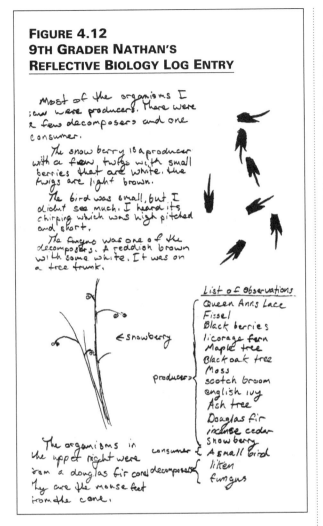

FIGURE 4.12
9TH GRADER NATHAN'S
REFLECTIVE BIOLOGY LOG ENTRY

Most of the organisms I saw were producers. There were a few decomposers and one consumer.

The snow berry is a producer with a few twigs with small berries that are white. the twigs are light brown.

The bird was small, but I didn't see much. I heard its chirping which was high pitched and short.

The fungus was one of the decomposers. A reddish brown with some white. It was on a tree trunk.

List of Observations
Queen Anns Lace
Fissel
Black berries
licorage fern
Maple tree
Black oak tree
Moss
scotch broom
english ivy
Ash tree
Douglas fir
incense cedar
Snow berry
A small bird
liken
fungus

← snowberry

producers

consumer

decomposers

The organisms in the upper right were from a douglas fir cone. They are the mouse feet from the cone.

The team co-wrote 10 pages of journal entries, complete with drawings of their observations, a map of the expeditions, and a chart showing the supplies taken and the money spent.

To assess her students, Cathy scored their reflective writing using the assessment list embedded in the Lewis and Clark Simulation Task Sheet (fig. 4.13) She reports that there were no arguments or disagreements over the earned scores because everyone knew beforehand how they were going to be graded. Fairness and consistency are critical to successful performance assessment.

Additionally, Cathy avoided group scoring dissatisfaction by using a Group/Self-Assessment chart (fig. 4.14, p. 79) for the Lewis and Clark Simulation. This assessment instrument asks for student input on how to evaluate individual learners' contributions to a group task. The groups decide who earns what.

We are excited about this student self-scoring instrument for cooperative effort. It offers great potential for us to solve the persistent problem of laggards in student groups.

Using Writing to Assess Students' Understanding Before Instruction

Although teachers typically use writing tasks as end-of-unit assessments or during-unit assessments, teachers may use them to assess student understandings *before* instruction begins. Just as visual representations—such as the Folded File Folder or concept maps (see Chapter 3)—are effective pre-assessments, so too can writing reveal to teachers what our students know in advance of instruction. Let's look at three useful mini-tasks.

The Picture Postcard

At the beginning of a unit or topic of study, teachers can "peek" into their students' existing knowledge base by asking them to jot ideas on a 5" x 8" index card. Students write what they already know or think they know about the topic. On the front side of the "postcard," students draw a picture of the topic.

When assessing student understandings at this early stage, teachers have a different objective than during or after instruction. This objective is to complete a preteaching diagnosis that determines: (1) the general level of content understanding and (2) any consistent misconceptions. The purpose is to inform the upcoming instruction rather than scrutinizing each student's level of understanding.

FIGURE 4.13
LEWIS AND CLARK SIMULATION TASK SHEET

Name _____ Date _____

Your group has been invited to become members of the Lewis and Clark Expedition. As a team you will simulate (1) keeping a travel journal of impressions of your experiences, (2) managing the supplies and money in an accounting log, and (3) creating a color expedition map documenting your journey.

The commander and second in command, Lewis and Clark, are ultimately responsible for documenting this expedition; however, they cannot succeed without your help and information.

Each group member should choose one of the following roles:
• The *topographer* keeps track of (sketches and describes in writing) the landscape and vegetation.
• The *surveyor* maps the journey—maintains the longitude and latitude of various locations along the journey—and records the climate, weather, and animals encountered.
• The *medic* maintains the health of the crew and learns as much as possible about Native American diseases and remedies.
• The *linguist* studies the cultures, languages, and customs of the native peoples you meet.
• The *quartermaster* maintains records of supplies and costs, solves problems, and records significant events.

This project is worth 100 points. Below is a breakdown of how to earn points. Read carefully and remember to strive to create work that is accurate, insightful, and complete.

Travel Journal   **50 Points**
The President of the United States, Thomas Jefferson, wants you to keep detailed records of the journey and what you learned:
• Turn in a neat-looking journal with at least five journal entries. These entries should correspond to the five locations labeled on your map (see map assignment in the final section).
• Date each entry.
• Note the longitude and latitude.
• Describe the terrain, vegetation, climate, and animals.
• Share any creative or exciting events that occur along the way.
• Include the different cultures, languages, and customs of the peoples you encounter.

The more detailed your journal entries, the better. Feel free to use pictures, descriptive language, and feelings in this journal.

Expedition Accounting Log   **25 Points**
Keep detailed records of the costs of the expedition:
• Maintain a chart showing supplies taken and money spent. Beside each item describe why you chose to take it.
• Describe the mode of transportation you selected and why, and keep track of transportation costs.
• Include your itinerary: your intended route, the number of days your journey will take, and your anticipated time of arrival.

FIGURE 4.13
LEWIS AND CLARK SIMULATION TASK SHEET *(continued)*

Expedition Map   **25 Points**
Create a color map of the expedition that contains:
• Five locations at which you stopped along your expedition.
• Major rivers, mountains, and so forth, labeled with their names.
• A marked route.
• A legend or key.
• A scale.

Agree on a plan that involves everyone equally in getting the work done. I will check in with your group every other day to monitor your progress.

- -

Detach this form, complete it as a group, and turn it into me by _____ . Under the header "Work Projects," list which of the above project parts each person will be working to complete.

Name	Role	Work Projects
	TOPOGRAPHER	
	SURVEYOR	
	MEDIC	
	LINGUIST	
	QUARTERMASTER	

Remember, you can all support one another in doing the work. There is always something valuable you can be doing with your time!

Therefore, creating a rubric, ChecBric, or checklist seems unnecessary to us. However, a teacher may want to consider using a Concept Acquisition Developmental Continuum (see Chapter 6, pp. 113, 120).

The Dear Teacher Letter

To check students' Info In knowledge before instruction, teachers may also use another writing task: the Dear Teacher letter. Students compose a short, friendly letter to their teacher announcing what they already know about the topic. To indicate their uncertainty about the accuracy of any of their content knowledge, they add a question mark (?). Likewise, students can mark certain pre-knowledge with an asterisk (*) to indicate what they think is especially important. Finally, in a P.S. to the letter, students inform their teacher what they hope will be covered in the unit, perhaps including a question or two they hope will be answered.

"Who's on First?"

A third assessment mini-task that occurs before instruction is "Who's on First?" This task, a combination of the written and visual modes, plays off a baseball metaphor. At four different times during a unit (the four bases), students reveal their current content understanding. The first time (first base) occurs before instruction. For example, at the start of a literature unit on the theme of survival, students fill out the worksheet shown in Figure 4.15 (p. 80).

A "Maxi-to-the-Max" Writing Task: The Civil War Newspaper

What about expanding the news article, a midi-task, into a maxi? Cathy Bechen, the middle school teacher referred to earlier, uses the desktop-published magazine performance task to measure her students' understanding of the Civil War. She, too, provides her students with a pre-task list of the five required ingredients: factual articles, interviews, letters to the editor, advertisements, and an illustrated cover.

Read this article, set back in 1860, about white Americans who fought against slavery, and ask yourself, Does this student understand abolitionism?

> The first thing you think about when reading the words "slave uprising" might be, "O.K., what Negro started it this time?" Actually, we do remember Nat Turner's famous revolt that claimed 57 lives, and the proud black American named Denmark Vessy, and other rebellious slaves.
>
> But what about white Americans who took a stand, and decided to fight for the freedom of slaves? There were different kinds of fighting, though. William Lloyd Garrison fought with his anti-slavery newspaper, *The Liberator*. He tried to make the Southern plantation owners realize that this was against God's ways. In his newspaper,

he "demanded to be heard." Garrison was considered very radical.

> Angelina Grimke Weld published a pamphlet called, "Appeal to Christian Women of the South." She was also considered a radical.
>
> Another way to fight was John Brown's way. He led an attack with 18 fugitive slaves on Harper's Ferry. Before he could go through with an ambush, he was caught, tried, and convicted for treason. John Brown was hung.
>
> These are acts of bravery. We should be grateful to them, and what they have done for us.

> *—Garrett*

The question, Does Garrett understand abolitionism? actually needs to be restated: To what *degree* does he understand abolitionism? And because he is using the Info Out mode of writing, we must ask, To what degree does he understand abolitionism, *and* how well does he write about it? Or consider Timothy's writing ability to hook readers' attention in this introduction to his factual article on Sojourner Truth:

> Ms. Truth, like most black women of our time [mid-1800s] started with humble if not horrible, beginnings.

Cathy decided to assess their writing using an adaptation of Oregon's Analytical Writing Traits Assessment. She opted to score for the original six writing traits, but to shorten the rubric into one page and use "kid-friendly" language. She used the six-point scoring scale shown in Figure 4.16 (pp. 81–82). This modified rubric is designed to assess students' use of the writing process. The fourth trait, ideas, may need to be reworked to add more content specificity. Cathy assigned each student in a group to write all four of the required pieces and to sign them, so she could assess each writer independently from his or her teammates.

She has also assigned the magazine writing task to assess her students on the topic of Westward Expansion. And, of course, magazines can be

FIGURE 4.14
GROUP/SELF-ASSESSMENT FOR LEWIS AND CLARK SIMULATION

Your group earned _____ out of the 100 points possible on your project. You know, better than I, who put out the most effort. I would like you to allocate individual points to your group members. Everyone in the group must agree with your allocations. You may not adjust any one person's points by a point value of more than 10. For example, if your group earned 90 points, one person could not get more than 100 or less than 80. If the group feels one person's score should increase by 7, another person's or persons' must decrease by 7.

Follow this step-by-step procedure:

1. Multiply your score by the number of people in your group. If you received a 90, and there were four in your group, that would equal 360 total points.

2. Next, determine if your group feels that anybody's score needs to change. This would happen if somebody didn't follow through with his or her part, or one person did all or more than his or her share of the work (map, journal, illustrations, research, chart).

3. Determine how much any person's score should increase or decrease. If one person's score moves up, that means he or she has put out a great deal of effort. It also means that someone else in the group should have done more, and that that person's score should decrease. If you increase one score by six, you must decrease another by six.

4. When you've finished, record the reason why the person received what he or she did in the "Reason for the New Score" column.

5. Add up your new scores. They must equal the number that you calculated in #1.

Name of Group Member	Score	Reason for the New Score
1.		
2.		
3.		
4.		
5.		
Total Score:		

FIGURE 4.15
"WHO'S ON FIRST?" PRE-ASSESSMENT FOR READING A NOVEL

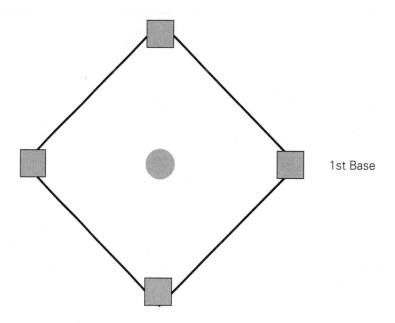

1st Base

Before we begin reading Gary Paulson's novel, *Hatchet,*[1] take a moment to reflect about your first thoughts.

1. Prediction: Why would a boy carry a hatchet with him on an airplane flight from his home in New York to Canada?

2. Tap prior knowledge: What do you already know about survival skills in the woods?

3. Author's writing craft: What do you like authors to do in their books that keep you interested and motivated to keep reading carefully?

[1]G. Paulson, (1987), *Hatchet,* (New York: Trumpet Club).

FIGURE 4.16
MAGAZINE EVALUATION SCORING GUIDE

Name _____ Date _____

1. Organization	1	2	3	4	5	6
You structure your ideas in a logical sequence. • Are your ideas, details, and examples presented in an order that makes sense? • How effective is your introduction? • Do you end your paper well?	Comments:					

2. Voice	1	2	3	4	5	6
You express ideas in an engaging and credible way. • Does your writing convey your personal voice? • Did you put something of yourself into the paper? • Is the writing lively? • Did you write what you really thought and felt?	Comments:					

3. Word Choice	1	2	3	4	5	6
You select words carefully to make your message clear. • Did you choose words that helped make your message both interesting and easy to understand?	Comments:					

A score of **6** means **exceptional**: my work is really great.
A score of **5** means **excellent**: my work is strong.
A score of **4** means **proficient**: my work is OK, and I am getting better all the time.
A score of **3** means **inadequate**: my work is weak but getting better.
A score of **2** means **limited**: my work is like that of a beginner.
A score of **1** means **missing**: I did not do this.

FIGURE 4.16
MAGAZINE EVALUATION SCORING GUIDE *(continued)*

Name _____ Date _____

4. Ideas	1	2	3	4	5	6
You communicate knowledge of your topic. • How well did you develop your ideas? • Did you know your topic well, and did you choose details that helped make it clear and interesting?	Comments:					

5. Sentence Fluency	1	2	3	4	5	6
Your paper is easy to read and understand. • Does it flow smoothly from one idea to the next?	Comments:					

6. Conventions	1	2	3	4	5	6
There are no glaring errors in writing conventions, and the paper is easy to read and understand. • Did you proofread carefully and correct spelling errors and punctuation?	Comments					

A score of **6** means **exceptional**: my work is really great.
A score of **5** means **excellent**: my work is strong.
A score of **4** means **proficient**: my work is OK, and I am getting better all the time.
A score of **3** means **inadequate**: my work is weak but getting better.
A score of **2** means **limited**: my work is like that of a beginner.
A score of **1** means **missing**: I did not do this.

handwritten instead of computer printed, and the topics certainly are not restricted to U.S. history.

Snapshot of Chapter 4

For centuries teachers have used writing to measure their students' understanding of what has been taught. Now, with performance assessment, we can fine-tune writing assignments and convert them into writing tasks that more accurately assess students' content knowledge.

In this chapter we have described the use of writing as an Info Out mode to assess student understanding. Writing performance tasks

• May be assigned before, during, and after instruction.

• Have a variety of purposes: to persuade, to explain/inform, to narrate a story, or to reflect on one's learning of content and/or process.

• Should offer a variety of audiences instead of the traditional teacher-as-sole reader.

• May be scored using a variety of devices, including a premade, generic rubric, such as the Oregon Department of Education's Analytical Traits (1996).

• Are strengthened and student performance improved when teachers provide students with task assignment sheets that preview the procedure, share the scoring device up front, and provide sample papers that model a range of performances.

By attending to these factors, teachers can serve as coaches who guide their understudies to higher and higher levels of performance.

What writing tasks have you used to assess your students' Info Out. Write to us. We would love to hear from you.

In the next chapter we consider using oral presentations in the same way.

5 Info Out: Assessing Students' Understanding Through Oral Presentations

➤ Info Out through three oral presentations
➤ Large-group formal speeches, small-group round-robin speeches, extemporaneous speeches, and press conferences
➤ The importance of substantive dialogue

Betty's Story:

Gilian, one of my 4th grade students, gave a speech to the class about library systems. She spoke articulately and precisely about the alphabetical system, the circulation system, and, in particular, the Dewey Decimal System. After her presentation, I asked her how she knew so much about the Dewey Decimal System. "I found it in the encyclopedia and copied it down," she said, "Then I memorized it and told it to the class." Hmmm . . .

What do we mean when we say "speaking"? In this chapter we intend to convince you that traditional oral reports are not an adequate means of assessing content knowledge; rather, if we are to fairly assess students' content acquisition, discourse—verbal *exchanges* between the student and others—must occur. We will describe three contexts in which these verbal exchanges are fostered:

1. Formal speeches in front of the class followed by questions and answers
2. Rotating small mini-speeches
3. Substantive dialogue between a student and the teacher

Students can use each setting to share the extent of their content knowledge with you. Additionally, we will

• Share some scoring mechanisms for assess-

ing these verbal exchanges
- Talk about the critical role questioning plays in prompting this dialogue
- Describe how these exchanges involve the use of key thinking strategies

What Do We Mean When We Say "Speaking"

Let's be clear. Children consistently use oral language as their primary vehicle for asserting, clarifying, and changing their perceptions and beliefs. Oral expression is "the core process in formulating and sharing human experience" (Marzano, et al., 1988). As Marzano and his colleagues state,

> It is a key pedagogical method because students who make meaning by stating academic knowledge in their own words demonstrate a depth of understanding well beyond what is reflected in recitation or in the recognition-testing of many paper-and-pencil tests.

In its simplest form, speaking can be defined as "saying words." However, when using speaking as a tool for assessment, most teachers prefer the more narrow definition of *public speaking*, that is, making a speech before an audience. Using this more narrow definition, assessment of speaking has tended to focus on the mechanics of giving the speech (delivery, organization, audience, etc.). For our purposes, we want to broaden the definition of "speaking" to encompass the larger concept of oral discourse. Oral discourse is verbal interaction at length about some subject—that is, content.

As noted, we'll look at three contexts in which speaking exchanges are fostered. Let's start at the end of a unit or course. We'll also discuss examples during and before a unit or course.

At the End of the Unit or Course: Speaking in Front of the Class

Most of us at some time or other have asked students to get up in front of the class and give an oral report on some subject. When scoring these presentations, most of us have focused on the features of the delivery of the speech and done little to score the content. How might a simple oral report assignment become a vehicle for students to demonstrate their content understanding? Here is how Betty adapted a traditional 2nd and 3rd grade oral report on animals to increase her ability to assess her students' acquisition of core knowledge content.

Speaking in Betty's Classroom at the Primary Level

Each year I assigned my young students a simple research project to gather information in the library on an animal of their choosing. I instructed each student to keep note cards on basic information about the animal and prepare a three- to four-minute speech to present in front of the class. The main emphasis of my instruction was on how to stand in front of the group, maintain eye contact, and project one's voice. Even though I gave students a short list of questions to answer, I did not focus on the content of the speech. I *did* focus on delivery and organization—making sure that my kids knew that a good speech had a beginning, a middle, and an end.

What were the results? I could not tell whether each student's content knowledge reflected simple memorization and regurgitation or actual concept development. In fact, as I listened to their animal speeches, I increasingly suspected they were reciting paragraphs directly out of the *World Book Encyclopedia*.

In the meantime, the Oregon State Content Standards were published. As I scanned the science section of the document, I noticed that, by the end of grade 3, my students would be expected to

• Identify examples of change over time

• Classify organisms based on a variety of characteristics

• Describe a habitat and the organisms that live there

• Identify daily and seasonal weather changes

I began to explore ways to adapt the oral report into a strong performance task that I could use to assess the above standards. Here is a synopsis of the task I created (see fig. 5.1). In the first assignment, I had included a list of questions for students to answer. However, in revising the task to better match the standards, I modified the questions. I also adapted the task and the scoring guide, (fig. 5.2, p. 91) to emphasize core content knowledge.

Speaking Assessment at the High School Level: The Debate

Another example of using speaking to assess core knowledge content comes from our colleague, Lilly Edwards, business systems teacher at Willamette High School in Eugene, Oregon. We have taken her basic idea and modified it slightly to enhance the scoring mechanisms. She uses this task with 11th graders in a business systems course. Part of their study includes social and environmental responsibility in business. This project, which includes a written paper and a debate, comes at the end of the business ethics study. In groups of four or five, students research a company that Lilly selects (fig. 5.3, pp. 93–94). She typically chooses companies that market high-interest products such as soft drinks and sports equipment. In the assignment for the oral presentation, two groups studying the same company argue in support of or in opposition to a company's environmental/social record.

As explained at the bottom of Figure 5.3, students assess their own work using the ChecBric (fig. 5.4, pp. 96–97), classmates assess their work also using the ChecBric, and each team conferences with the teacher to come up with a grade for the project. Lilly uses a unique system to determine the scores for all members of each group. This system, the Peer Evaluation Scoring Guide, is shown in Figure 5.5 (p. 98).

Of course, we have chosen to detail the oral component here—the debate rated in the last column (p. 98). However, remember we mentioned earlier that students, as a part of the whole culminating project, were expected to discuss/brainstorm, conduct research, produce a work plan, and write a report in preparation for the debate.

One last point: we don't do full-blown oral presentations all the time. Realistically, we try to incorporate only a couple of these more formal oral presentations throughout the year because of obvious time constraints.

Round-Robin Mini-Speeches in Larry's Middle School Class

During a study of U.S. history in the 1800s, I offered my students a menu of topics to choose from for a research project. Realizing that we didn't have time for an in-depth study of all the topics of this historical period, I opted for the "divide and conquer" approach. Each kid would become a mini-expert on a topic and then teach classmates what he or she had learned.

After my students indicated their first, second, and third topic choices, I paired them to learn about the topic using resources such as their history textbook, a supplemental text, and the Internet. Before the pairs began their research (Info In), I told them what the Info Out was going to be. Each team would create a visual representation of newly learned content information in the form of a graphic organizer on 11" X 17" paper. (See Chapter 3.) This graphic organizer would then serve as a prompt for a five-minute mini-speech to a small

FIGURE 5.1
PRIMARY-LEVEL ANIMAL ORAL REPORT TASK SHEET

Name _____ Date _____

Here is your task:

A. Select an animal from the following list. You should select an animal that you find interesting and that you would like to learn more about.

Frog	Spider	Chick	Bear
Butterfly	Cat	Dog	Bird
Whale	Pig	Lamb	Fish

B. Find out as much as you can about the animal you have selected. Get information from at least three different books, magazines, or people. Our media specialist will also help us learn how to use the World Wide Web to get more information.

C. You will receive four note cards. On each note card copy these focus questions:

Card 1. How does this animal's looks **change** from when it is a baby until it becomes an adult?
Card 2. Where is this animal's **habitat**? What does this animal's home look like?
Card 3. What does this animal **eat** when it is a baby? When it is young? When it is an adult?
Card 4. What does this animal do in different **seasons** (spring, summer, winter, and fall)? How does the animal **change** based on the weather?

As you find out more about your animal, write notes about what you learned on the note cards.

D. Prepare a speech about your animal. The speech should be about 3–4 minutes long. Use the information on your note cards to create your speech. Your speech will be scored on three parts:

Knowledge:	**How much did you learn about the animal?**
	• Can you answer the focus questions listed under letter "C"?
	• Do you include the answers to your questions in your speech?
	• Can you answer questions from the audience?
Delivery:	**How well do you present your speech in front of the class?**
	• Do you look at the audience?
	• Do you speak up enough so that everyone can hear?
	• Do you speak at a good rate, not to slowly or too fast?
	• Do you say your words clearly?
Organization:	**Is your speech organized?**
	• Does your speech have a good beginning?
	• Do your ideas make sense and flow from one to another?
	• Do you end your speech well?

FIGURE 5.1
PRIMARY-LEVEL ANIMAL ORAL REPORT TASK SHEET *(continued)*

E. When you give your speech, it is OK to use props to help you. You may want to show a picture of your animal that your found or drew. You may also refer to your note cards to remind yourself of what you want to say. But you should not read your speech.

F. You will need help. What kind of help is OK? It is OK to have someone help you read and discuss what you read. It is OK for someone to listen to you practice your speech and give you feedback on how to improve it. You should take your own notes.

G. Your speech needs to be completed and ready to give by _____. I will check in with you on the following days to see if you are getting parts of your work completed. These dates are important:

Date: _____   You have selected an animal to study.
                        You have copied the questions on the note cards.

Date: _____   You have gathered information and recorded it on the note cards.

Date: _____   You have a speech prepared and are practicing giving it.

Date: _____   You give your speech in front of the class.

Take this sheet home, and read over it with your parents. Complete the bottom of the form, tear it off, and bring it back to school tomorrow.

✄✄✄

Name _____   I have selected this animal to study for
                                           my oral report: _____

Student Signature   Parent Signature

_____   _____

Check any of the following supplies you may want to get from school:
_____ a large sheet of butcher paper   _____ scissors
_____ a set of felt-tip pens   _____ tape
_____ a set of colored pencils   _____ books, magazines

group of classmates who would rely on them for learning about the topic.

When the class found out that the Info Out was an oral presentation, they displayed what could be described as major signs of displeasure. But their concerns were largely mitigated upon learning that the oral presentation would be made to a small group and that everyone would be working with a partner.

I also told them that they would repeat their mini-speech to four small groups that would rotate from team presentation to team presentation. This repetition would help them become increasingly comfortable presenting in front of a group. To clarify what I meant, I drew a picture of how the classroom would be set up to accommodate this round-robin oral performance task.

I was pleasantly surprised at how well they accomplished the rotations. As I circulated the room, sitting in on all four groups, three things impressed me. First, I liked how each pair of speakers used their graphic organizer as a cue card for the mini-speech. I was also pleased with the partners' ability to share the speaking load. (I had told them that they had better both contribute.) Third, I was thrilled at the small group audiences' behavior. They were attentive, polite, and seemingly interested in the content material.

Of course, I was wise enough to assist the audiences in how to listen properly. I had distributed small booklets of blank paper for required note taking at each rotation. The kids were to begin each booklet page with the title of the topic and the two speakers' names. Then, as the mini-speeches progressed, they jotted down notes, wrote questions, and/or drew quick illustrations to facilitate their Info In from their classmates.

Day 2 also went very well. Four new pairs of students were stationed at the four presenter tables armed with their graphic organizers. I split the remaining students into four rotating audiences that spent five to seven minutes with each pair of presenters taking notes and asking follow-up questions. I, too, circulated during all four presentations, so that I could assess the oral Info Outs. At the end of Day 2 eight presentations had been completed (with two kids on each team), so we were halfway home.

Day 3 didn't go as well. Perhaps I should have given the class a break from the activity, or maybe it was the bad luck of the draw that two of the four presenter pairs were jokers—and irreverent jokers at that! For example, the pair presenting on Lewis and Clark were less than inspiring: they failed to mention the reason for the expedition, its main effect on the development of the United States, and even the role of Sacajawea (Sacagawea). They did, however, reveal to their antsy audience that "Lewis and Clark were cool dudes who kicked b_ _ _ when faced with danger." Good to know.

Possible Pitfalls

As with any assessment task, pitfalls loom before us. The above description of the Lewis and Clark fiasco discloses the most dangerous potential problem: lack of content expertise. If students are supposed to reveal their understanding of new content information (Info Out), then they had better do a good job of learning it (Info In). The graphic organizer mini-task worked for most teams, but obviously not all.

Next time I will work with several teams—whom I suspect might need it—for a quick assessment of their graphic organizer before they make their oral presentation. This added step should improve quality control. And quality is essential: not only for the two presenters, who need to learn about their topic, but also for the audiences, who count on them for quality teaching.

Another pitfall I quickly identified was how rushed I was in moving among and scoring four presentations (times two presenters) during each 50-minute class period. If the task's scoring device has more than just a few traits to assess, then it's doubtful that it can be done. I suggest that if you use this round-robin approach that you score just two traits:

    1. *Delivery:* oral communication ability to have an impact on your audience.

    2. *Content:* shared expertise of key points of your topic.

    Of course, you could give each audience member a copy of the scoring device (like one created from the above two traits, or the one Lilly or Betty used earlier) for peer evaluation. The problem becomes what to do with the peer data. In the "outside" chance that you receive some inappropriate or outrageous comments, simply scan the stack before handing the feedback over to the presenter. Some teachers aggregate the peer review scores and incorporate them into the overall. We have, on occasion where appropriate, asked other adults (university student volunteers, trained community members, for example) to give feedback, which we have incorporated into the grade. However, we don't make it a practice to incorporate student feedback as a part of the overall grade. If you have had experience in this area and would be interested in sharing it with us, please give us your thoughts.

    With students listening to four oral presentations each day, a third pitfall involves the danger of their losing track of all this new content information Although the note-taking requirement in the booklets was a stroke of genius for focusing students' intake of information, too much content was still being shared for significant processing and remembering to occur.

    To assist in the latter, I altered the presentation schedule by beginning each class period with a review session. I asked the kids to open their note-taking booklets to a particular topic from the day before, and highlight with a colored pen or pencil the two to three facts they believed were "important enough to remember into adulthood." I then led a class discussion on their highlighted notes to gain consensus on the key points.

    This exercise improved my students' Info In by giving them a chance to "Repair" their initial note taking. Some kids had missed key points; others had tried to record everything the presenters had stated. I suspect that this Repair activity improved their note-taking skills. Having a daily review slowed down the schedule, but it was well worth it.

    Naturally, I collected all note-taking booklets to assess the audience's listening and processing ability. I did not have a scoring device for this assessment, so I merely assigned points. Next time I intend to use Tim Whitley's "Post-it" technique. (See Chapter 4, pp. 72, 74.)

Speaking During a Unit or Course

We want to suggest a few possibilities for using speaking as an assessment during a unit or course. One easy way to assess content knowledge acquisition during instruction is for students to share a two- to three-minute extemporaneous speech on the subject at hand. This activity will quickly give you a picture of each student's current thinking. Ask students to respond to one or two questions. To do so, list each student's name on a 3" by 5" index card, and randomly draw out two or three names to present on the topic when you lack time to listen to everyone. For some reason, we have noticed that students tend to be more attentive when they know that the teacher is making an effort to check in with everyone randomly.

    Another of Betty's favorite during-unit oral assessments is what we call the "Home Improvement" Triangle. Most students are familiar with the popular television series, "Home Improvement." As a class we discuss the various characters in the situation comedy and how they think and communicate about various subjects. The three characters we develop are shown in Figure 5.6 (p. 99).

    Students are asked to assume one of these

FIGURE 5.2
SAMPLE SCORING GUIDE FOR PRIMARY-LEVEL ANIMAL
ORAL REPORT

Name _____ Date _____

Knowledge About My Animal

	I told what my animal looks like as an adult.
	I told what my animal looks like as a baby to show how it changes over time.
	I told where my animal lives and what its home is like.
	I told what my animal eats when it is a baby, when it is young and when it is an adult.
	I told what my animal does in different seasons (spring, summer, winter, and fall) and how it changes based on the weather.
	I answered questions from the audience.

Delivery

	I looked up at the audience.
	I spoke loud enough for everyone to hear.
	I spoke clearly.
	I spoke at a good rate, not too fast or too slowly.

Organization

	I had a good beginning to my speech.
	My ideas made sense and flowed one to the other.
	I had a good ending for my speech.

+ = I did a really great job in this area.
✓ = I am doing OK in this area.
− = I need to work on this.

three characters and speak to the topic at hand from that person's point of view. Each student can then shift into another character and describe the content from that character's point of view; for example, from Tim's point of view, from Al's point of view, and then from Mr. Wilson's point of view.

Speaking Before a Unit or Course

For us, the most effective way for students to share their content knowledge through speaking at the beginning of the course is by conducting a press conference. Work through key focus questions (see Chapter 2), and give students an opportunity to make opening remarks about their current thinking on the question. Then have the audience, as the press corps, ask follow-up questions in a popcorn fashion—popping around the room randomly and asking questions.

Substantive Dialogue

It is important to note that in some cases, you may not be clear about students' content understanding even after examining their work produced in the activities described earlier. For all students—and *in particular* for these students—it is imperative that you engage them in "substantive dialogue," our third format for speaking. We have found this format particularly appropriate with kids at both ends: special education and talented/gifted students.

What we call "substantive dialogue" Fred Newmann (1991) refers to as "substantive conversation." For authentic student achievement to occur, he says, substantive conversation must be present. That is, when assessment of content acquisition is the goal, substantive conversation between the learner and some supportive resource—teacher, critic, or other knowledgeable authority—is necessary.

Working from Newmann's constructs, we suggest that substantive conversation is present when

• Two or more people engage in sustained, continuous talk.

• There is considerable interaction about ideas related to the subject at hand.

• The talk is not scripted or controlled—the course of the conversation is less predictable than in conventional classroom exchanges.

• The conversation builds coherently on the student's ideas through the teacher/expert/critic's use of questioning prompts.

• The student is able to deal with the knowledge hierarchically from specific facts, concepts, and generalizations, to applying these concepts in other contexts.

Facilitating Substantive Dialogue

How might teachers engage students in substantive dialogue? Consider using a series of questioning prompts tied to specific thinking strategies. Students cannot show what they know about a topic without "thinking" about that topic. In particular, thinkers use

• Focusing strategies
• Remembering/retrieving/summarizing strategies
• Analyzing strategies
• Generating strategies
• Evaluating strategies

Figure 5.7 (p. 100) lists these strategies, their purposes, and appropriate questioning prompts (Marzano et al., 1988). Remember, when you ask salient questions about the topic, you force students to use one of these thinking strategies. So, not only do you as the assessor get a better picture of what students understand, but you are giving them practice in improving their thinking!

FIGURE 5.3
BUSINESS SYSTEMS SOCIAL AND ENVIRONMENTAL RESPONSIBILITY PROJECT

Name _____ Date _____
Members of my group are _____
My group will research this company _____

Research
Each person in your group will research this company in order to answer the following questions:

1. What do we mean when we say *social responsibility? Environmental responsibility?*

2. What does this company manufacture and market?

3. What is its gross sales and profit for the last five years?

4. How many employees does the company have?

5. How does the company operate (franchise, public corporation, etc.)?

6. Who owns the company? What other companies does it own?

7. Where is the company located, and is it a local, regional, national, multinational company?

8. Is this company socially responsible? Why or why not?

9. In this company environmentally responsible? Why or why not?

After completing your individual research, you can work together as a group to combine and strengthen your ideas for your upcoming team debate on this company. You must be prepared to speak either in support of or in opposition to the company's environmental and social record. You will need to cite a minimum of *five* sources in support of your position. You must also cite a minimum of *five* sources to discount or refute that position.

FIGURE 5.3
BUSINESS SYSTEMS SOCIAL AND ENVIRONMENTAL RESPONSIBILITY PROJECT *(continued)*

Oral Presentation
The day before your presentation, the flip of a coin will determine which team will speak in the affirmative and which team will speak in opposition. The presentation format will be as follows:

Both Teams: Respond briefly to the above questions 1 through 7 to introduce the rest of the class to your company (6–7 minutes).

Team One: Present your case citing sources to show that this company is environmentally and/or socially responsible (5 minutes).

Team Two: Present your case citing sources to show that this company is not environmentally and/or socially responsible (5 minutes).

Team One: Refute the arguments of team two and reinforce your position (3 minutes).

Team Two: Refute the arguments of team one and reinforce your position (3 minutes).

Team One: State your conclusions (3–5 minutes).

Team Two: State your conclusions (3–5 minutes).

Both Teams: Respond to questions submitted by the audience (6–7 minutes).

Completing This Work
You will complete this project over the next three weeks, working both in class and outside of class.

Everyone in your group *must* participate in the debate by presenting at least one point or counterpoint. You will also be expected to respond to questions from the teacher about your sources: where you found them, whether they are primary or secondary sources, and whether you consider them to be reputable.

You will be given time to work in the library here at Willamette High School and in the library at the University of Oregon. You will also have an opportunity to pursue information on the World Wide Web. Your team must develop a plan for using your group time and for recording and organizing your data.

Scoring Your Work
Your work will be scored in three ways:
   1. You will evaluate your own work by completing the attached ChecBric [fig. 5.4].
   2. Your classmates will evaluate your work using the ChecBric.
   3. Your team will conference with the teacher, working from the Peer Evaluation Scoring Guide (fig. 5.5, p. 98), to determine a grade for the project.

Scoring All Three Types of Oral Presentations

We imagine that you are all sitting back thinking, "Larry and Betty, get real! No way do I, nor any other teacher I know, have time to pull off the oral presentation assessments that you are suggesting." Believe us, we understand. We have been hard pressed to do so ourselves. We have had to make a number of time-saving adaptations in order to survive. These adaptations include:

1. For efficiency, scoring the task during the presentation instead of waiting for a postpresentation conference.

2. On occasion, videotaping the presentations and having students review the tape to score their own work.

3. To prevent teacher and listener burnout, having only two or three students give their presentations each day, thus extending the assessments over a couple of weeks.

4. Training a cadre of adult volunteers to help you score student oral presentations.

Betty's Core Content Cadre

So—you ask—how do you train adults to score student presentations? When I train students to use the speaking scoring guides shown earlier, I invite a core of parents and other adult volunteers to join us for the same training. At an after-school follow-up session, I give the adults time to practice scoring as needed to increase reliability. When your district provides training in scoring for teachers, I would suggest that you invite adult volunteers to the inservice session too.

Originally, when asking other adults to participate in substantive dialogue with students about their work, I had trouble helping them know how to score the work. So I developed a Substantive Dialogue Scoring Guide (fig. 5.8, pp. 101–102). Participating adults simply select one or two prompts from each area in the left column to ask students and then record a few phrases that illustrate student responses in the second column. Next, using something like the Generic Rubric for Declarative Standards developed by Marzano, Pickering, and McTighe (1993), they can assign an overall score.

Of course, you can customize the questions for the specific task at hand and coach your scorers, as needed, in how to use the scoring mechanism. Because we are just beginning to try out this mechanism, we haven't worked out all the bugs yet. If you try it, let us know via the Web how it works and if you needed to make any adaptations.

Yes, But . . . Significant Effects and Adaptations

When designing performance task assignment sheets and scoring mechanisms, it is important to pay attention to some significant effects and adaptations. Here are a few to note.

Constructing Answers for Students: When you engage in substantive dialogue with one or more students, the kinds of questions or prompts you provide will shape the responses you receive. That is, occasionally we have found ourselves prompting students in such a way that indicated not only the *type* of response we were looking for, but the *content* of the response, as well. For example, when interviewing students, you might be tempted to ask, "What evidence can you list that clearly shows us that the XYZ Corporation is socially responsible to its subcontracted employees?" From our point of view, this type of prompt tends to push the student toward a particular point of view. Teachers must guard against "leading the witness." A better prompt would be, "What evidence from your analysis supports the notion that XYZ treats its subcontracted workers fairly or unfairly?"

The Broadside-of-the-Barn Effect: When constructing a scoring mechanism for assessing content knowledge, it is very easy to make the question prompts and scoring guide traits so

FIGURE 5.4
SOCIAL AND ENVIRONMENTAL RESPONSIBILITY PROJECT CHECBRIC

Name _____ Date _____

Check the appropriate column: yes or no. Then give yourself one overall score from 6 to 1 in the bottom "Overall Score Box." A score of **6** equals a strong performance; a **1** represents a weak performance.

Content

Yes	No	
		Were the focus questions answered in the presentation?
		Were five sources identified in support of/in opposition to the issue?
		Were responses to the opposing arguments handled well?
		Were the ideas supported adequately by evidence?
		Was research evident, or was the presentation based upon personal experience and supposition?
		Were questions from the audience handled well?
		Overall Content Score

Organization

Yes	No	
		Could the main ideas be easily identified?
		Was the presentation put together in such a way as to make it easy for the audience to understand?
		Were details placed in the speech for optimum impact?
		Did the presentation have a credible introduction?
		Did the presentation have a strong conclusion?
		Overall Organization Score

FIGURE 5.4
SOCIAL AND ENVIRONMENTAL RESPONSIBILITY PROJECT CHECBRIC *(continued)*

Language

Yes	No	
		Was language carefully selected to emphasize the main points and impress the audience?
		Were the usage and grammar correct?
		Was concise, vivid, and varied language used?
		Overall Language Score

Delivery

Yes	No	
		Was eye contact maintained throughout the presentation?
		Was the use of gestures, movements, and other nonverbal techniques effective?
		Did the presenters speak clearly and fluently?
		Overall Delivery Score

---

explicit that you get what we call leading-the-witness or paint-by-number responses. Formula questions can lead to formula responses as demonstrated above.

On the other hand, when working with younger students we feel justified in being more explicit about what we are after, so that students can learn how to respond to these kinds of assessments. In other words, design the scoring guide for younger students so that their target is the "broadside of the barn," so they have a very good chance of hitting it. As they mature, they should be hitting ever smaller, more focused targets.

Confusing Reading for Speaking: Some folks would hold that students must write out their oral presentations word for word before presenting them to the group. In our experience, many students resort to writing the report and reading it. Reading is *not* speaking. Students need to be able to differentiate using props from reading canned scripts. We want to know how well a student can talk on his or her feet about the subject—not memorize and regurgitate canned knowledge.

Snapshot of Chapter 5

In this chapter we introduced you to our third Info Out mode—oral presentations. Simply speaking in front of a class, we emphasized, is not an adequate means to assess core content knowledge acquisition. We discussed the importance of oral dis-

FIGURE 5.5
PEER EVALUATION SCORING GUIDE

Name _____ Date _____

As an individual complete this chart. First list the names of those persons in your group on the left. Then as-sign each person a score from 1 to 4 in each area identified. The score should reflect your perception of that person's contribution to the group work. Be sure to include yourself on the chart. Your individual responses will not be revealed to the others in your group.

I will take the charts from all group members and summarize the results before I conference with you as a group. At that time we will review the ChecBric scores from yourself and others, along with this Peer Evalua-tion Scoring Guide, and agree on an appropriate grade for each team member.

Use the following scoring guide to assign points:

4 = Was very helpful, had great ideas, made important contributions, readily volunteered to do work, and always carried through with the work.

3 = Was helpful, had good ideas, made helpful contributions, volunteered to do work, and consistently carried through with the work.

2 = Was a little helpful, contributed some ideas, and did some work.

1 = Was not helpful, did not share ideas, made no contribution, did not carry through with work.

Name	Brainstorming Discussions	Research	Development of a Work Plan	Written Report	Debate

course as your main vehicle for doing so.

We then introduced you to several possibilities for assimilating oral discourse/substantive dialogue after, during, and before unit assessments. They included the "Home Improvement" Triangle, round-robin mini-speeches, and press conferences.

We also suggested that you increase the amount of substantive dialogue that occurs in your classroom by training your own personal CCC—Core Content Cadre—who, working from a Substantive Dialogue Scoring Guide, engage all students in substantive oral discourse.

Here are some questions you may want to consider about the information in this chapter.

Please send your ideas to us via our ASCD web site.

• How could I go about creating my own CCCs?

• What are some other ways to increase the amount of substantive dialogue in my classroom?

• Are the thinking and questioning prompts described here useful? Can I expand them and improve them in some way?

Where are we on our assessment journey? We have now addressed Info Out through the use of visual representations (Chapter 3), written performances (Chapter 4), and Oral Presentations (this chapter). Next we turn our attention to large-scale "maxi-to-the-max tasks."

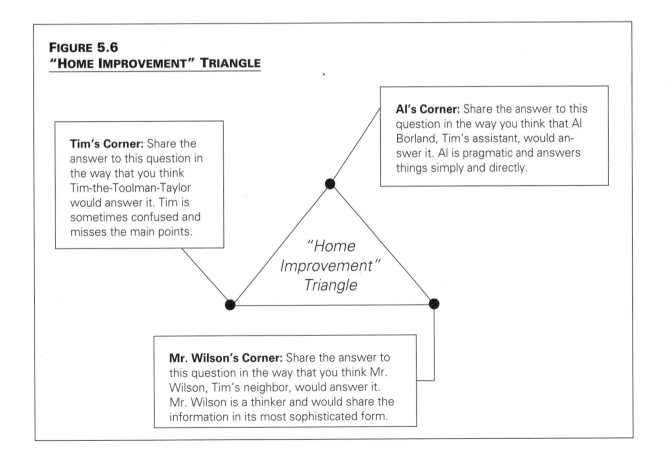

FIGURE 5.6
"HOME IMPROVEMENT" TRIANGLE

Tim's Corner: Share the answer to this question in the way that you think Tim-the-Toolman-Taylor would answer it. Tim is sometimes confused and misses the main points.

Al's Corner: Share the answer to this question in the way you think that Al Borland, Tim's assistant, would answer it. Al is pragmatic and answers things simply and directly.

"Home Improvement" Triangle

Mr. Wilson's Corner: Share the answer to this question in the way that you think Mr. Wilson, Tim's neighbor, would answer it. Mr. Wilson is a thinker and would share the information in its most sophisticated form.

FIGURE 5.7
THINKING STRATEGIES AND QUESTIONING PROMPTS

Thinking Strategy	Question Prompts
Focusing Strategies are used to selectively attend to information.	• What subject/topic will we be discussing? • Did you identify any problems? • What is most important to understand about your topic? • What are the key points about your topic?
Remembering/Retrieving/ Summarizing Strategies are used to store and retrieve information.	• In your own words what did you learn? • What can you remember about ___? • How would you describe ___? • If you could use three or four sentences to pull this all together, what would you say? • Overall, what is the situation?
Analyzing Strategies are used to examine parts and relationships, compare and contrast, and facilitate perspective-taking	• How is ____ like or different from ____? • What are the attributes of ___? • How is ___ an example of ___? • What evidence can you list for ___? • What is your point of view about this? • Are there other points of view about this subject?
Generating Strategies are used to produce new information, meanings, or ideas.	• How would you create/design a new ___? • What solutions would you suggest for ___? • What ideas do you have to ___? • If you were ____ how would you have handled ____?
Evaluating Strategies are used to assess the reasonableness and quality of something.	• What do you think about ___? Why? • Which ____ is most significant and why? • What are your sources? • How do you know they are credible? • Did you detect any biases? • What criteria did you use to come to this conclusion?

FIGURE 5.8
SUBSTANTIVE DIALOGUE SCORING GUIDE

Student _____ Date _____ Rater _____

Thank you for helping to assess each student's core knowledge understanding through *substantive dialogue*.
A. Select and use one or two of the question prompts in each area.
B. Highlight those used and then jot notes on the student's responses.
C. Score the work using the four-point scale developed by Marzano, Pickering, and McTighe[1] (p. 102).

Question Prompts	Student Responses
Focusing: • What is the subject/topic we will be discussing? • Did you identify any problems? • What is most important to understand about your topic? • What are the key points about your topic?	
Remembering/Retrieving/Summarizing: • In your own words what did you learn? • What can you remember about _____? • How would you describe _____? • If you could use three or four sentences to pull this altogether, what would you say? • Overall, what is the situation?	
Analyzing: • How is _____ like or different from _____? • What are the attributes of _____? • How is _____ an example of _____? • What evidence can you list for _____? • What is your point of view about this? • Are there other points of view about this subject?	
Generating: • How would you create/design a new _____? • What solutions would you suggest for _____? • What ideas do you have to _____? • If you were _____ how would you have handled _____?	
Evaluating: • What do you think about _____? Why? • Which _____ is most significant and why? • What are your sources? • How do you know they are credible? • Did you detect any biases? • What criteria did you use to determine this?	

FIGURE 5.8
SUBSTANTIVE DIALOGUE SCORING GUIDE *(continued)*

General Comments:

_____

_____

_____

_____

Overall Score: _____

4 = Demonstrates a thorough understanding of the generalizations, concepts, and facts specific to the task or situation and provides new insights into some aspect of this information.
3 = Displays a complete and accurate understanding of the generalizations, concepts, and facts specific to the task or situation.
2 = Displays an incomplete understanding of the generalizations, concepts, and facts specific to the task or situation and has some notable misconceptions.
1 = Demonstrates severe misconceptions about the generalizations, concepts, and facts specific to the task.

[1]R.J. Marzano, D. Pickering, and J. McTighe, (1993), *Assessing student outcomes, Performance assessment using the Dimensions of Learning model* (p. 30), (Alexandria, VA: ASCD).

Info Out: Assessing Students' Understanding Through Large-Scale Projects or Performances

➤ Info Out through the construction of substantive projects or performances
➤ Concept Acquisition Developmental Continuum
➤ Consensus Definition
➤ UmbrellaTella
➤ Project Criteria and Scoring Guide
➤ Museum Exhibit Assessment List

Betty's Story:

I watched as the judges made their way to my spot at the 7th grade science fair. I anxiously stood to the side of my homemade telegraph machine. The first judge approached me and asked, "Tell me about your telegraph. How does it work?" I stuttered and finally uttered something like, "Well, my dad helped me make it, and I think he said it works like this . . ." Even though I had actually done most of the construction myself (with elaborate coaching from my dad), I had absolutely no

idea how it worked. But it sure looked great! And I am proud to announce that I turned it in on time. But unfortunately, I did not have a clue about the basic concepts involved in telegraphy.

Another Betty Story

A few years ago I was packing for a speaking engagement. It was about 11 p.m., and I was preparing to fly out the next morning. As I rushed around the house gathering materials and organizing my overhead transparencies, my 9th grade son approached me, "Hey Mom! You remember that big science project I need to do?" I asked, "You mean the one where you run a classic scientific investigation, track your data, and write up the results?" "Yeah, that's the one. Well, I need to get started because it's due tomorrow. I need your help." Enough said.

Why Some Large-Scale Projects Fall Short

So what do these stories have to do with performance tasks? These kinds of performances—science fairs, exhibitions, and other elaborate productions—have been around for years. Many schools have long histories of incorporating culminating projects at the end of substantive courses of study. However, these types of projects have been known to generate a number of negative phenomena including:

• *The Razzle Dazzle:* The performance has a lot of flash but no substance.

• *The Parasite:* The parents pick the topic. The student may do the work but has no interest or ownership in the project. Moms or Dads, however, get to live out their dreams/interests/fantasies through their child's performance.

• *Scaffolding:* The student picks a project of personal interest, but may not do any of the actual work. It is difficult to determine how much scaffolding (shoring up) by others (usually parents) occurred.

• *The Fizzle:* Not enough guidance or direction is provided. The task is assigned, and students are expected to miraculously produce a fantastic project in six weeks. They rarely do.

• *The Celebration:* This category results from an erroneous belief that performances should be showcases—festivals, parties, or other gala

events—without evaluation. Everyone should be honored—no matter the quality of the work.

• *The Uneven Playing Field:* Some students draw from many resources (e.g., parents, computers, libraries, and art supplies) in creating their projects, while other students draw from few or no resources.

• *Near Death:* Teachers, near exhaustion, walk around school with glazed-over eyes mumbling, "Why did I do this to myself? I will never do this again!" Some refer to this as the "Homer Simpson" Effect.

Given the negative effects associated with these types of tasks, can the construction of large-scale projects or performances serve as an effective Info Out mode? We hold that they can and should be one critical form of evaluation—a form in which students "pull it all together." As teachers, then, how do we frame the production of models, displays, projects, or other elaborate performances to (1) minimize the above-mentioned effects and, at the same time, (2) maximize the opportunities for students to explicitly reveal their understanding of core knowledge? And how might we evaluate the quality of these performances?

We call these large-scale tasks Substantive Synthesis Projects and define them as maxi-tasks in which students use a combination of key Info Out processes (writing, speaking, and graphic representations) to synthesize and extend their learning through producing or constructing a large-scale project.

In this chapter we will show you how traditional large-scale projects can be converted into Great Performance tasks. We will also describe how to create an audience for the task and how we host such events in the classroom, at the school or district level, and in the community. To do this we will use several examples.

Developing Great Large-Scale Projects and Performances

Our goal is to construct an end-of-unit substantive project or performance that incorporates our definition of a Great Performance task plus a few other traits critical to the success of substantive projects. Figure 6.1 provides a description of these traits.

Because teachers appreciate a step-by-step approach in developing a task, we want to familiarize you with the 10-step task design process we use. We used it in developing the examples in previous chapters.

1. Be clear about your targets: the skills and knowledge students will demonstrate and the standards you expect them to meet.

• Most performance tasks will include a process standard (such as speaking, writing, or composing) and a core content knowledge standard (such as the concept of separation of powers in a democracy or the concept of form in the arts).

• You may work from your state department of education's content and performance standards, your district standards, or various national standards projects to identify specific standards to target.

• It is possible to connect a few targets, but don't try to make it the "mother of all tasks" in which students are held responsible for too many targets at one time.

• Begin by asking yourself, What knowledge and skills will students develop and demonstrate through this task?

2. Be familiar with the critical process traits and key content concepts of a strong performance.

• When eliciting performances of key processes (speaking, writing, problem solving, etc.), examine the scoring guide to familiarize yourself with the critical traits that must be present in a performance. Work from existing scoring guides or construct one unique to this task.

• When eliciting performances of core knowledge concepts, develop a set of key questions, the answers to which will elucidate key conceptual understandings. Answer the questions yourself to identify the key points students will need to make.

3. Create and describe a context in the task that will make it meaningful and engaging.

• The context should be of interest to students.

• The context should clearly elicit performances related to the targets.

• The context can be an important issue, situation, question or integrating theme that will engage students' interest.

• The task should be authentic (replicate as nearly as possible what a real-world performance would entail). To be authentic, tasks need not always be set in the real world, but should involve students in experiences and processes that simulate those of practitioners in the field.

• The performance should have a wider audience than just the teacher; that is, someone outside of class who would find the work meaningful.

4. Write a short description of the task.

• Incorporate the key questions into the task statement as appropriate.

• Include critical traits from the scoring guide as appropriate.

5. Rewrite the task in a clear and concise manner.

Use language that will clearly specify the various ways that students might communicate about or exhibit their conclusions. Also, be as specific as possible about the parameters in which students must complete the task. List any criteria related to

• Information sources (required number, notes, bibliography, use of particular references, etc.)

• Time elements (date final project due, date individual components due, etc.)

• Collaboration/assistance (working

FIGURE 6.1
KEY ELEMENTS OF LARGE-SCALE GREAT PERFORMANCE TASKS

Content Standards:	The task targets a combination of process and core knowledge content standards.
Elaboration of Core Knowledge Content:	The task facilitates the development of expertise through the synthesis and application of core knowledge content.
Application of Key Processes (Graphic Representations, Writing, Speaking, and Constructions):	The task uses key Info Out processes in combination to get students to reveal their current construction of content knowledge.
Explicit Scoring System:	The task is evaluated with an overt scoring system shared with students up front.
Audience Larger Than Just the Teacher:	An engaging and authentic context is created for the task in which someone would be interested in the work besides the teacher or parent.
Student Choice:	The task allows for student preferences to a greater extent than other types of tasks previously described.
Contract:	Students and parents sign a contract specifying that the project reflects the work of the student.
Work Plan:	The teacher provides students with a step-by-step plan for accomplishing the task within given time periods.
Student Self-Reflection:	Students are required to produce a reflective journal and "processfolio." The processfolio is a collection of all of their work—the final product, the drafts, sketches, revisions, and so on.

---

alone/with others, how many, reporting individual contributions, parental/other adult involvement, etc.)

• The presentation of the project (size of display area, whether an oral presentation is required, appropriate labeling, written description, etc.)

6. Assign the task to students.

• Identify or construct scoring guides/rubrics for the standards you are going to assess.

• Discuss the task in class, and answer any questions.

• Distribute a task sheet to students. Post copies of the task sheet, the scoring guide, and work plan in the classroom.

7. Develop a step-by-step work plan with the class.

• The work plan should provide students with guidance and assistance in completing the project.

• Break the task into parts, and delineate the sequence in which various parts are to be completed.

• You may want to have students keep a "processfolio." A processfolio is a collection of all of their work—notes, drafts, final products, and so forth.

• If necessary, specify what kinds of help parents and other adults can give.

8. Strive for excellence.

• Show samples of excellent work as models.

• Reinforce with students the developmental process of creating multiple drafts/trials/attempts ("repairs"), with each subsequent draft representing work of higher quality.

• Throughout the process, give students opportunities to reflect on their work and how to improve it.

9. Provide instruction.

• Offer instruction that supports the development of necessary knowledge and skills, and coach students toward effective performances.

• Throughout the completion of the task, conduct formative evaluations of students' progress through observation, examination of documents, and student self-assessment. Use this information to give students feedback on how to improve their performance before the due date.

10. Score the task and make necessary revisions.

• Use the scoring guides to give students feedback on how their overall performance on the task reflects mastery of the content standard benchmark.

• If possible, join with other teachers to score a number of the tasks together. Doing so will allow all of you to calibrate your scoring with one another and to clear up any questions that may arise from the responses.

• It may be helpful to create a common form on which to record your feedback. In some cases the scoring guide itself provides room for comments.

• To be efficient, some teachers make initial judgments about the performance as students present their work in class, followed by a short teacher-student conference.

• Take the time to identify the rubs in the task, and note any changes that need to be made for next time. If you wait until later, you will forget.

An In-Class Large-Scale Performance: The Homelessness Task

Let's walk through these 10 steps creating a sample substantive synthesis project, a large-scale maxi-task for 7th and 8th graders that could be adopted to use at the high school level. We'll have students produce a traditional research report and oral presentation assignment within the context of this maxi-performance task. The issue will be the growing homeless population in Eugene, Oregon.

We should note that in our district teachers are not assigned particular topics to teach in a specified time frame but, rather, are given major conceptual themes to develop within particular courses. Each teacher then has some flexibility in selecting topics as vehicles to develop particular concepts. Teachers are able to tap into lively, contemporary community issues if desired. You may not have that much flexibility. As we work through this task, examine how you might adapt the idea to your own setting.

1. Be clear about your targets: the skills and knowledge students will demonstrate and the standards that they will be expected to meet.

Our local newspaper had been carrying a series of articles on homelessness. Some folks had suggested that the city and county should work cooperatively to find a location for a "car camp," an area where the homeless could camp in their automobiles throughout the winter. One suggested location was a parking lot next to a community science and technology museum frequented by school children. A number of citizens, assuming that the homeless were dangerous, objected to this location. Of course, this objection led to heated debate about the characteristics of homeless people. The letters to the editor of the local paper were full of stereotypical depictions of the homeless.

At the same time, we were exploring ways that we could teach to the state content standards in the social sciences. Two 8th grade targets (benchmarks) for social science content are:

• Identify multiple causes of a single event, and explain how a single event can impact more than one sphere of human activity.

• Describe change and continuity over time within the following content theme: economic and technological developments and their impact on society.

We knew students had had opportunities to demonstrate their understanding of these concepts in relation to historical events such as the Civil War and the development of industrial America. We wondered whether we might use the homelessness issue to bring the concepts to life in the present. Could the topic incorporate the depressed timber economy in the Northwest and its impact on maintaining housing for unemployed families?

In addition, we identified these 8th grade benchmark content standards in writing, speaking, and social science analysis. You could identify similar standards from your own state and district curriculum frameworks or from national curriculum standards.

Writing

• Convey clear, focused main ideas with accurate and relevant supporting details appropriate to audience and purpose.

• Demonstrate organization by developing a beginning, a middle, and an end with clear sequencing of ideas and transitions.

• Use complex sentences to increase variety in sentence structure.

• Use correct spelling, grammar, punctuation, capitalization, paragraphing, and documentation.

• Use a variety of modes (e.g., narrative, imaginative, expository, persuasive) and forms (essays, stories, business memos or communica-

tions, research papers, technical reports) to express ideas appropriate to audience and purpose.

Speaking

• Convey clear, focused main ideas with accurate and relevant supporting details appropriate to audience and purpose.

• Demonstrate organization by developing a beginning, a middle, and an end with clear sequencing of ideas and transitions.

• Use descriptive and accurate words appropriate to audience and purpose.

• Demonstrate control of eye contact, speaking rate, volume, enunciation, and gestures appropriate to audience and purpose.

Social Science Process: Analysis

• Compare data to determine differences of fact and opinion in clarifying an issue.

• Explain an event or issue from two or more points of view, and explain why perspectives among individuals and groups vary.

• Describe short- and long-term consequences of alternative courses of action.

2. Be familiar with the critical process traits and key content concepts that must be present in a strong performance.

We set about examining our state rubrics (called "scoring guides" in Oregon) in writing, speaking, and social science analysis to be clear about what traits to teach and assess in each performance. As referenced in Chapter 4, in Oregon we work with an analytical trait assessment scoring guide for writing that includes the following traits:

• *Ideas/Content:* The paper shows clarity, focus, and control. Key ideas stand out and are supported by details.

• *Organization:* The paper shows effective sequencing. The order and structure of the text move the reader through it.

• *Sentence Fluency:* The sentences enhance the meaning, and the writing has a flow and rhythm to it.

• *Conventions:* The writing reflects the control of standard writing conventions such as grammar, paragraphing, punctuation, and capitalization.

• *Voice:* The writing is expressive, engaging, and sincere. It reflects an awareness of the audience.

• *Word Choice:* The words convey the intended message and a rich, broad range of words are used.

• *Citations:* References to sources are noted in the text. If appropriate, a bibliography is attached.

Our speaking scoring guide includes the following traits:

• *Ideas/Content:* The communication is clear and focused. The speaker has a clear purpose in speaking, and the main ideas stand out.

• *Organization:* The speaker uses effective sequencing suited to the purpose. The speech has an effective beginning, body, and ending.

Teachers in our district created the following traits when assessing social science analysis:

• *Knowledge of the Topic:* The key questions are clearly addressed in the paper and oral presentation. The student can identify substantive themes and issues related to this topic.

• *Issue Analysis:* The speaker examines multiple perspectives on this issue and uses critical thinking in the analysis.

• *Action Proposal:* A position is taken, supported, and clearly communicated. Relevant actions are proposed.

We could have searched our state content standards and probably identified a number of other targets to incorporate into this task. But we realized that we had too many already. We have found that students cannot attend to a lot of traits *and* do a credible job. And teachers lose their san-

ity in trying to teach to and assess each trait! The list above (social science, writing, and speaking) has worked for us because we have a long history of working with the analytical trait assessment in writing and speaking. Students at this level come to us with some familiarity with the traits. You may need to zero in on a smaller combination of social science core knowledge content and writing or speaking—or focus on just one area as you get started.

To help students examine the relevant facts, concepts, and generalizations related to the topic, we generate some key focus questions to be addressed in the task (as introduced in Chapter 4). There is no magical number of questions, and both you and your students can generate them. Here is a list of questions around the concepts of cause and effect, change, and continuity using the content topic of homelessness.

• How has homelessness changed over time in Eugene?

• What are the causes of homelessness?

• What effects does homelessness have on the individual, the environment, and the community?

• What are the characteristics of life for homeless teens?

• Who are the interested parties in this situation, and what are their points of view on a solution?

• What are the strengths and weaknesses of each of these proposed solutions?

• What solution do you propose to address this issue and why?

3. Create and describe a context for the task that will make it more meaningful and engaging.

We like to begin by identifying an important issue or situation within the school, community, or national context—as a possible starting point for producing a performance. For example, students might explore:

• Is the playground equipment inadequate?

• Should popular à la carte menus be changed in middle school cafeterias to incorporate more nutritious foods?

• Is homelessness a problem in our community?

4. Write a short description of the task.

At this stage you as the teacher/assessor make a first attempt to put your main ideas on paper. Your description needn't be elaborate. Here is our First Dare:

> *Is homelessness a problem in Eugene? Some people are telling the city council that it is becoming a large problem. The council has asked you to investigate this issue. You will work in small collaborative work groups to study homelessness in Eugene, Oregon. Your group will need to write a technical report and make a speech about this important issue.*

5. Rewrite the task in a clear and concise manner.

Use language that clearly specifies the various ways that a student might communicate about or exhibit his or her conclusions. Be sure to include any parameters you want included in the performance. Here is our Repair:

> ### Homelessness Task
>
> *Some people are telling the city council that homelessness is becoming a large problem in Eugene. The council has asked you to investigate this issue. You will be working together on a team with three other students. You will need to apply the problem-solving/decision-making process and the writing process to formulate a systemic citywide proposal/plan to address this issue.*
>
> *On ____(date)____ representatives of the city council and the city staff will give you an opportunity to share your proposal. You will have 20 minutes to present your proposal orally, followed by 15 minutes in which you will be expected to respond to questions.*
>
> *Your proposal may take any format that*

you decide is appropriate. You will also submit your proposal in writing and provide copies for all representatives. Make sure you answer the following key questions in your written work and presentation:

> • *How has homelessness changed over time in Eugene?*
> • *What are the causes of homelessness?*
> • *What effects does homelessness have on the individual, the environment, and the community?*
> • *What are the characteristics of life for homeless teens*
> • *Who are the interested parties in this situation, and what are their perspectives on a solution?*
> • *What are the strengths and weaknesses of each of these proposed solutions?*
> • *What solution do you propose to address this issue, and what is the reasoning in support of your proposed solution?*
>
> *Be sure to include a reference list that identifies your information sources.*
>
> *Attach a one-page description of your collaboration that describes how you accomplished this task and how you worked together to complete it. Also, as individuals, complete the attached scoring guide. When you complete the project, score your work. I will then conference with you and score your work also.*

6. Assign the task to students.

As with every task, we give students a copy of the task assignment and scoring guides at the beginning. We review the task as a class and post it somewhere in the room. At the start of each subsequent class period, we discuss class and individual progress and provide tips to those who need to get to work. Students are constantly directed to the team work plan checklist presented in Figure 6.2 to monitor their progress.

7. Develop and distribute a scoring device and a step-by-step work plan.

In this and previous chapters we have described a number of useful scoring devices. Later

FIGURE 6.2
A TEAM WORK PLAN

Names of Group Members _____

_____

_____

_____

Please work from this worksheet as you complete the homelessness project. On the following dates, you will be expected to conference with the teacher and review your work. When you have completed a task, all group members should place their initials in the second column. In the third column assign your group a score from 1 to 6. Assigning yourselves a score of 1 means that you think your work in this area is very poor. Assigning yourselves a score of 6 means that you, as a group, agree that your work in this area is excellent.

Date Due	Initial When Complete	Score	Tasks to Be Completed
			Group Work Plan • Describe how you have assigned jobs. • Share the agreements that you have made about the storage of materials and supplies. • Describe the decision-making process your group will be using to complete the work.
			Information Gathering/Group Process Check In • Turn in a rough draft of the answers to the questions. • Provide an oral status report on your group work. • Brainstorm a format for your oral presentation.
			Next-to-Final Draft • Turn in your next-to-final draft of the written proposal. • Turn in an outline of your oral presentation. • Provide an oral status report on group work.
			Final Presentation • Make your oral presentation and present your written proposal. • Turn in the written description of your group collaboration. • Turn in your processfolio and individually completed scoring guide.

in the chapter we summarize them in Figure 6.12 (p. 135). Select, adapt, or develop a device to use for this task. Our repeated experiences with students who are unable to manage a large-scale project to meet deadlines have convinced us that a work plan is *absolutely* necessary. We sense that many of you are nodding in agreement. A work plan provides the needed structure for the work to be accomplished and gives the teacher planned opportunities to assess student work throughout the process.

8. Provide work samples to show students what "good" looks like.

We use student work from year to year as models with our current classes. These examples help students to visualize what a strong performance might look like. Additionally, we provide examples of less-than-excellent work for students to critique. When no student samples are available, we create samples ourselves. If we are pressed for time and can't create our own, we scan the local news sources for examples. We collect opinion editorials and letters to the editors from our local paper, and we occasionally video- or audiotape debates, forums, and other performances from the nonprint media. These examples show students what works and what doesn't work.

9. Provide instruction.

Let's walk through several instructional methods that could be used to teach and assess "before, during, and after" acquisition of core knowledge concepts (cause and effect, change and continuity) using the topic of homelessness.

Consensus Definition

One method that we have used successfully, the Consensus Definition, is from our friend Nancy McCullum, a gifted teacher who is now a principal. Students write a short definition of the concept being explored, in this case, homelessness. Then they pair with one or two others and construct a group definition.

This is a great time for you to stroll around the room collecting anecdotal records on students' initial perceptions. Judi Johnson—our friend and an extraordinary teacher in Sun River, Oregon—suggests photocopying sheets of address labels with a different student's name on each label. Attach the sheet to a clipboard, and carry it around with you as you observe. Jot notes onto each individual's labels and date them. After class, you can affix these note labels to wherever you keep anecdotal records. This system also enables you to notice which students you need to observe. As you remove labels, you will consciously attend to those students whose labels are left on the sheet.

When creating a Consensus Definition, we instruct students that our goal is a two- or three-sentence statement that defines the concept. As a class, all small groups share their definitions, and the class comes to agreement on one definition. Posted in the classroom, this definition becomes the working definition for the study. Throughout the unit students can suggest modifications and revisions.

UmbrellaTella

From that definition, we can begin to explore the related concepts through a method we call UmbrellaTella. Using UmbrellaTella is a way to graphically represent the relationship of larger "meta" concepts to their related subconcepts and topics.

When using the UmbrellaTella with younger students, we bring an umbrella into the classroom, record the concept name and definition on strips of paper, and attach them to the main fabric of the umbrella with safety pins. It works better if the umbrella is large and has a number of metal spokes. Our goal is to hang several related subconcepts and facts to each of the metal tips around the umbrella's edge. We do this by

- Giving students a copy of an umbrella on a sheet of paper.
- Asking them to examine each key question and jot down quick answers to each question on the strips hanging from the umbrella.
- Partnering students with one or two others who then create group answers to each key question and record them on larger card-stock sentence strips.
- Sharing each group's sentence-strip answers with the whole class. (At this point, no judgments are made about the accuracy or quality of the responses.)
- Clustering similar sentence strips and attaching them all to the UmbrellaTella near the metal tips. Older students may work from the paper diagram of the umbrella rather then a real one.

Throughout the unit, as students acquire new content understanding through Info In of reading, listening, viewing, or manipulating (see Chapter 2), allow them to remove, revise, and recreate sentence strips for the UmbrellaTella. Figures 6.3 and 6.4 show how an 8th grader completed an UmbrellaTella before unit instruction about watersheds and, later, during instruction. At the end of the unit, each student can complete an UmbrellaTella to summarize what he or she has learned.

10. Score the task, and then make necessary revisions.

Figure 6.5 (pp. 117–118) shows the scoring guide (rubric) we constructed for this homelessness task. Of course, we drew from the existing state scoring guides but adapted it with student-friendly language.

This then becomes an ideal time—while the problems with the task are fresh in your mind—for making any necessary revisions. While scoring the tasks, you may want to ask yourself:

- Did the students' performances reveal what they were intended to reveal?

- Did the scoring device accurately measure student performance?
- Did the task sheet and the work plan adequately prepare the students for the performance?
- What improvements could be made? What revisions are necessary?

Concept Development à la Developmental Continuum

The more we have worked with assessing concept development, the more intrigued we have become with the notion of creating a developmental continuum to assess content acquisition. This continuum tracks a student's development of conceptual understanding from *novice*—with no conceptual understanding—to *expert*—able to present a superior degree of breadth and depth of information on the subject. In creating this continuum, we crafted language based on our own experience as well as Bloom's Taxonomy of Cognitive Objectives (Bloom, 1956). (See fig. 6.6, p. 120).

You may ask students to self-reflect on their stages of concept development and rate themselves using the continuum. You may also want to use this continuum as the "ideas and content trait" on a rubric with other traits. Or you might monitor each student's concept development progress over time as students move through a number of units.

Your Turn: What Do You Think?

In summary, the Homelessness Task incorporates the following assessments:

- For Core Knowledge Concepts

Before and During: Anecdotal records and informal interviews related to student work using the Consensus Definition and UmbrellaTella methods.

After: The content of the position paper using the Concept Acquisition Developmental Continuum.

FIGURE 6.3
AN 8TH GRADER'S UMBRELLATELLA ABOUT WATERSHEDS BEFORE INSTRUCTION IN THE UNIT

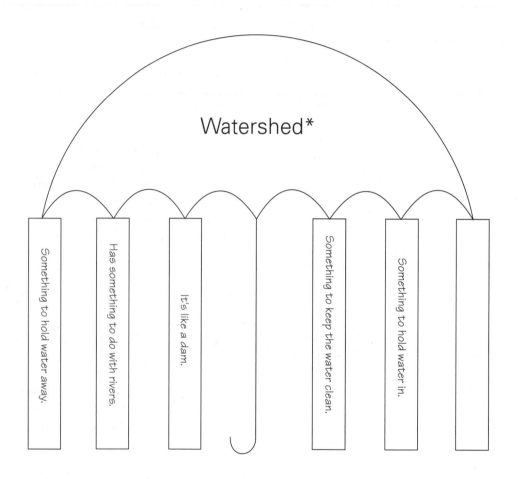

Watershed*

Something to hold water away.

Has something to do with rivers.

It's like a dam.

Something to keep the water clean.

Something to hold water in.

*The concept is recorded here. Students record a two- or three-sentence definition on a sentence strip and attach it here.

Students record answers to the key focus questions on the hanging sentence strips. They revise, edit, or replace them with more accurate statements.

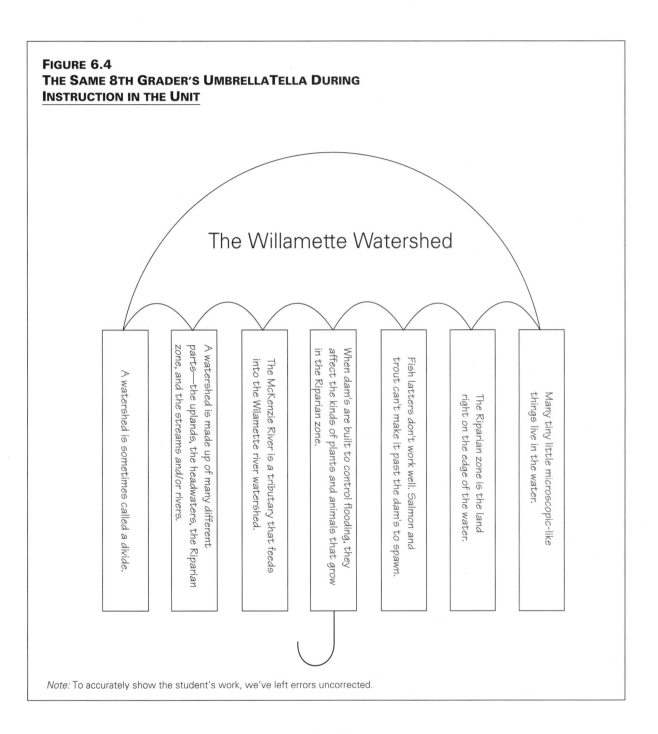

FIGURE 6.4
THE SAME 8TH GRADER'S UMBRELLATELLA DURING
INSTRUCTION IN THE UNIT

The Willamette Watershed

A watershed is sometimes called a divide.

A watershed is made up of many different parts—the uplands, the headwaters, the Riparian zone, and the streams and/or rivers.

The McKenzie River is a tributary that feeds into the Willamette river watershed.

When dam's are built to control flooding, they affect the kinds of plants and animals that grow in the Riparian zone.

Fish latters don't work well. Salmon and trout can't make it past the dam's to spawn.

The Riparian zone is the land right on the edge of the water.

Many tiny little microscopic-like things live in the water.

Note: To accurately show the student's work, we've left errors uncorrected.

• For the Writing Process
Before, During, and After: Analytical trait assessment using the Homelessness Project Rubric.

• For the Speaking Process
During and After: Analytical trait assessment using the Homelessness Project Rubric.

• For Social Science Analysis
After: Analytical trait assessment using the Homelessness Project Rubric.

From your point of view, does the homelessness task measure the intended core knowledge outcomes of cause and effect, change and continuity, and the process standards in writing, speaking, and social science analysis? In what ways could you adapt this task for use in your classroom? Did you find anything particularly intriguing about the task or scoring mechanisms?

A County-Level Maxi-Task: The Student Achievement Convention

We designed the homelessness task as one form of large-scale culminating performances to share in class with invited guests. Our next example is a model for a maxi-*out-of-class* exhibition for use with K–12 students at the school level, at the district level, and, in this case, at the county level. The Student Achievement Convention idea was developed by Marilyn Olson and Kermit Horn formerly at our countywide Lane Education Service District (1200 Highway 99 North, Eugene, OR 97402). Each year the convention offers students from Lane County public schools an opportunity to provide evidence of academic achievement in three areas:

1. The *Project Fair* includes presentations of the processes and products of in-depth learning experiences.

2. The *Portfolio Exhibition* contains collections and reflective evaluations of selected works that show individual achievement and progress toward specific goals and standards.

3. The *Video Festival* features original video productions.

How the Convention Works

From January through April each year, teachers introduce the convention events to students, students select topics, and then they develop projects, videos, and/or portfolios. Each Lane County school is assigned a number of spaces (1 space per 100 students enrolled). By the first of April schools are expected to submit an "intent to participate" form. If a school chooses not to participate, other schools are assigned their spaces.

By the first of May schools must also submit a list of judges—one judge for each one or two projects. Judges can be teachers, parents, community members, or administrators. The first day of the convention, judges receive specialized instruction in using the scoring rubrics and conducting interviews with students. It is interesting to note that, year after year, a number of retired folks return to judge at the convention along with teachers and parents. What a great way to help inform our retired community about what is going on in schools!

The three-day convention is held at our county fairgrounds exhibit hall the third week of May. The first day, Tuesday, students set up their projects in the morning. Each project, portfolio, and video is judged in the afternoon by at least two judges, and major scoring discrepancies are settled by a third party.

School children from around the county are scheduled to visit the convention on Wednesday and Thursday. In addition to viewing their fellow students' projects, portfolios, and videos, these children may enroll in other special events such as a science celebration, star lab, and young writers' workshops offered simultaneously in other areas of the fairgrounds. Let's examine the Project Fair portion of the convention in more detail.

FIGURE 6.5
HOMELESSNESS PROJECT RUBRIC

Please rate your performance using a six-point scale. The teacher will conference with you and also assign a score in each area.

1. **Position Paper**

My Scores	The Teacher's Scores	The Trait
		Word Choice • Your words convey the intended message. • You use a rich, broad range of words.
		Sentence Fluency • The sentences you chose enhance the meaning. • Your paper has a flow and rhythm to it.
		Conventions • You demonstrated that you use standard writing conventions appropriately (grammar, paragraphing, punctuation, capitalization).
		Ideas/Content • You present your ideas with clarity, focus, and control. • Your main points stand out.
		Organization • You use effective sequencing in your paper. • The order and structure move readers easily through the text.
		Voice • Your writing is expressive, engaging, and sincere. • Your writing reflects an awareness of your audience.

2. **Oral Presentation**

My Scores	The Teacher's Scores	The Trait
		Content • Your speech is clear and focused. • You made your purpose clear, and your main ideas stand out. • You effectively use visual tools to share information.
		Organization • You use effective sequencing suited to your purpose. • Your speech has an effective beginning, body, and ending.
		Language • You effectively use speaking conventions. • Your words are specific and accurate.

FIGURE 6.5
HOMELESSNESS PROJECT RUBRIC *(continued)*

2. **Oral Presentation** *(continued)*

My Scores	The Teacher's Scores	The Trait
		Delivery • You maintain effective eye contact. • The rate at which you speak and the volume you use are appropriate

3. **Overall Content Knowledge and Social Science Analysis**

My Scores	The Teacher's Scores	The Trait
		Knowledge About Homelessness and Related Issues • You address the key questions in your presentations. • You identify substantive themes and issues.
		Issue Analysis • You examine multiple perspectives on the issue. • You use critical thinking to analyze the issue.
		Action Proposal • You take, support, and communicate your position. • You propose relevant actions that can be implemented.

Scoring Scale

6 Exemplary   Your work at this level is both exceptional and memorable. It shows a distinctive and sophisticated application of knowledge and skills.

5 Strong   Your work exceeds the standard. It shows a thorough and effective application of knowledge and skills.

4 Proficient   Your work at this level meets the standard. It is acceptable work that demonstrates application of essential knowledge and skills. Minor errors or omissions do not detract from the overall quality.

3 Developing   Your work at this level does not yet meet the standard. It shows basic, but inconsistent application of knowledge and skills. Minor errors or omissions detract from the overall quality. Your work needs further development.

2 Emerging   Your work at this level shows a partial application of knowledge and skills. It is superficial (lacks depth), fragmented, or incomplete and needs considerable development. Your work contains errors or omissions.

1 Not Present   You presented no work in this area.

Creating and Evaluating Project Fair Entries

The Project Fair gives students an opportunity to exhibit a major learning experience that combines content knowledge with process skills to produce a product, a portfolio, or a video that demonstrates their learning—what we call a large-scale maxi-performance task. Each project is evaluated by two judges who look for and score three specific traits described on the scoring guide:

1. Topic and treatment
2. Learning development and process
3. Presentation/communication

Each participant is expected to complete an exhibit with an accompanying project notebook, as well as participate in an information presentation and interview. Figures 6.7 and 6.8 show, respectively, the Project Fair Guidelines and Participation Checklist (p. 121) and the Registration Form (122–123). Judges score students' work using the Project Criteria and Scoring Guide shown in Figure 6.9 (124–129).

A sampling of projects submitted for the 1997 Project Fair included:

• Nitrate Contamination of Groundwater from Fertilizers (grade 10)
• How Hiccups Happen (grade 3)
• Dams: Pros and Cons (grade 7)
• Hidden Lessons: A study of Gender Bias in Our Schools (grade 10)
• What Attracts Bees? (grade 5)

What kind of scoring mechanism is the Project Criteria and Scoring Guide? We refer to it as a "Scorecard Rubric." The Scorecard Rubric has a number of attributes of a rubric (analytical traits, descriptors, and scoring scale), but it adds an additional feature, a total overall score—a feature that middle and high school teachers particularly like. This total score enables them to convert the scores into percentages for calculating letter grades.

A Community-Based Substantive Synthesis Performance Task: From a Drop of Rain

Let us shift our attention to an extensive, elaborate, large-scale project where the audience is the whole community. This project, "From a Drop of Rain: A Tale of Two Rivers," is currently in its third of four years. At the end of the third year, the project produced a six-month-long museum exhibit April through September at the University of Oregon Museum of Natural History. We share this maxi-to-the-max task as another example of a large-scale performance task that is suitable for grades 6 through 12. We don't want to scare you off with the magnitude of the project. You can, of course, make modifications, adjustments, and reductions as you choose.

A Tale of Two Rivers is a hands-on, field-based project in which secondary students from three school districts studied watershed ecosystems, stewardship, and natural resource management. The project is centered within the Willamette Valley of central Oregon on the main stem of the Willamette River and one of its major tributaries, the McKenzie River. Students are conducting field studies at diverse sites within this watershed region.

Students, teachers, and administrators from six middle schools and two high schools are participating. Each school has a core team of three to five teachers, two parents, and five students to steer the project. In the first year, each of the eight schools selected a site to explore and study within the McKenzie and Willamette River systems. Together, these sites represented the richness of the watershed as a whole. For example, they included

• The oldest state-owned fish hatchery in Oregon
• The largest complex of native prairie remaining in western Oregon

FIGURE 6.6
CONCEPT ACQUISITION DEVELOPMENTAL CONTINUUM

Read the continuum[1] from the bottom to see a progression of concept acquisition.

Stage Seven: Expert	• In presenting a breadth and depth of relevant and accurate facts, concepts, and generalizations about the subject, the student focuses on substantive themes, problems, and issues. • The student analytically evaluates the information and makes qualitative and quantitative judgments about the subject according to set standards. • The student synthesizes and extends facts, concepts, and generalizations about the subject to solve problems, develop position papers, and the like, requiring original, creative thinking. • The student effortlessly presents acquired knowledge about the subject in a number of different forms moving from concrete to abstract. • The student is able to clearly articulate his or her point of view if appropriate. • The student clearly shows original thinking and creativity in approaching the data and in presenting it to others.
Stage Six: Accomplished	• The student presents a breadth and depth of relevant and accurate facts, concepts, and generalizations applicable to the subject. • The student investigates the subject through an analysis of its component parts. • As appropriate, the student identifies interested parties and presents their multiple perspectives on the subject. The student articulates and evaluates the reasoning, assumptions, and evidence supporting each perspective. • The student begins to show original thinking in approaching the data and in presenting it to others.
Stage Five: Progressing	• The student demonstrates comprehension of pertinent facts and concepts applicable to the subject by drawing data from a variety of sources including primary and secondary sources. • The student begins to demonstrate an understanding of principles, laws, and theorems related to the subject. • The student interprets information and solves simple problems using the information.
Stage Four: Developing	• The student presents some relevant and accurate information (facts, rules, or details) applicable to the subject. • This information is based on fact as well as increasingly informed opinion. • If the student presents an argument, it is weak or implausible. • Where issues exist, the student is able to identify the central issue but states it in general terms. • The student is capable of changing information given by the teacher into a different symbolic form.
Stage Three: Beginning	• Information is based on a narrow frame of reference and uninformed opinion and is from a limited number of sources. • The student presents irrelevant, simplistic, or inaccurate information about the subject.
Stage Two: Readiness	• There is an attempt to address the subject; but no detail is provided/no breadth of information is present.
Stage One: Not Present	• The student presents no information about the subject. There is no attempt to address the subject in any meaningful way.

[1] We want to acknowledge the work of George Westergaard, social studies teacher at South Eugene High School, who has worked with his advanced placement students in using similar content continuums.

FIGURE 6.7
STUDENT ACHIEVEMENT CONVENTION

Project Fair Guidelines and Participation Checklist
Lane County Education Service District
Eugene, Oregon

The **Project Fair** provides an opportunity for students to display a major learning experience that combines content knowledge with process skills to produce a product or demonstration of learning. All projects[1] will be evaluated by a judging team trained to look for and score these specific project elements:

- Topic and Treatment
- Learning Development and Process
- Presentation/Communication

Careful presentation of the following items will help judges identify the purposes and strengths of a project:

A. PROJECT NOTEBOOK:
___ 1. *The Registration Form* (two copies)

___ 2. *Progress Journal:*
Record daily any ideas, thoughts, observations, questions, resources, problems, impressions, or discoveries you encounter while working on the project. Sketches, diagrams, data tables, photographs, or other information important to the project are encouraged.

___ 3. *Annotated Resource List:*
Include books, magazines, experiences, equipment—anything that contributed to the success of the learning experience—and tell how each was successful.

___ 4. *A Self-Evaluation of the Project:*
Use the scoring guide to assess elements of the learning experience and to comment on academic benefits. (See Project Criteria and Scoring Guide [Fig. 6.8].

___ 5. *Optional Letters of Support:*
Parents, teachers, or others who are aware of the effort and progress of the student(s) involved in the project may add their comments and commendations.

B. EXHIBIT:
___ The process, products, and results important to the project are displayed visually in a 40"x30"x73" space. This exhibit may take any combination of forms—display, video, final report, model, and so on.

C. INFORMATION PRESENTATION AND INTERVIEW:
___ Student should come prepared to talk with judges and explain how the project was chosen, the learning processes and procedures used, the important outcomes, and the learning value of the project.

For *group projects,* all group members should complete a journal and self-evaluation explaining their interest and involvement with the project.

[1]Projects may be entered for display only and will not be judged.

FIGURE 6.8
STUDENT ACHIEVEMENT CONVENTION

Project Fair Registration Form
Lane County Education Service District
Eugene, Oregon

Submit two copies per project.[1]
Due May 13, 1997, at the time of registration.

This form is completed for each project, and two copies are placed in the front of the project notebook.

Project Title _____ Registration No. _____
                                                                (assigned at registration)

Class/Subject _____

Project Duration   *Date Started* _____ *Date Completed* _____

Student/Group _____ Grade _____
                                                   (List all students. Use back if necessary.)

Teacher _____ Phone _____

School _____ District _____

In registering this project for the Project Fair, we agree to the following (check each item that is true):

_____ 1. All guidelines for the Project Fair (specified on the Student Achievement Convention Project Fair Guidelines and Participation Checklist [fig. 6.7]) have been met, including completion of the self-evaluation Project Criteria and Scoring Guide [fig. 6.9].

_____ 2. We have arranged for the project to be set up by 12 noon, May 13, 1997, and removed following the Awards Reception, Thursday evening, May 15, 1997.

_____ 3. One or two students will be available for an oral interview about the project between 1:30 and 3:30 p.m. on May 13, 1997.

_____ 4. We accept full responsibility for security of the items displayed.

_____ 5. The work on this project has been done primarily by the student(s).

FIGURE 6.8
STUDENT ACHIEVEMENT CONVENTION REGISTRATION FORM *(continued)*

I grant my permission to the Lane County Education Service District and _____School District to release my child's name, photograph, address, and any other information about him or her for public information purposes to the extent in such manner and for such public information as deemed appropriate by the Lane County Education Service District and _____ School District. Parents/Guardians will be informed of each release.

Signed _____   Date _____
　　　　　　　　　　(Parent/Guardian)

　　　　　　　　　　　　　　　　　　　　　　　　　　　　Phone _____

Signed _____   Date _____
　　　　　　　　　　(Student)

Signed _____   Date _____
　　　　　　　　　　(Sponsoring Teacher)

Signed _____   Date _____
　　　　　　　　　　(School Principal)

[1]Two copies are required because one copy is displayed with the project, and when students remove their displays, this copy goes home. The other copy is filed with the project fair staff in case there are challenges to the awarded scores.

• The largest population of western pond turtles

• Several water resource management projects

• The settlement of the Willamette Valley's earliest human residents, the Calapooia peoples

• High-use recreation areas

• Sites requiring restoration because they play a critical role in providing basic community needs (i.e., electricity and water)

• Sites that provide enjoyment to a vast number of residents and visitors, and are greatly valued by local communities

Targeting 6th through 12th grade students, the project has been a springboard for school districts to develop career paths for students interested in careers in natural resource management. One of its great strengths is the active participation by more than 20 community agencies and organizations that provided technical expertise and advice via e-mail and in the field.

A major goal of the project is to apply concepts in natural resources settings and create products that benefited the community, such as nature trails, interpretive guides, or research findings.

A Dream Becomes Reality

As teachers and agency folks brainstormed possibilities, several potential studies emerged.

FIGURE 6.9
AN EXAMPLE OF A SCORECARD RUBRIC
THE PROJECT CRITERIA AND SCORING GUIDE FOR THE LANE COUNTY PROJECT FAIR

I. Topic and Treatment: What did you study, and how well did you learn it?

Score	A. The project provides opportunity for important and challenging learning.				
	5 = outstanding	4 = • Evidence of real interest. • Sense of ownership. • Topic/purpose well stated. • Wholehearted effort. • Represents new area of learning.	3 = balance	2 = • Lacking interest, challenge. • Routine response. • Purpose unclear. • Halfhearted effort. • Familiar, easy topic. • Compliance without commitment.	1 = incomplete

COMMENTS:

_____

_____

_____

Score	B. Project outcome provides evidence of detailed, deep thinking about the task or topic.				
	5 = outstanding	4 = • Factual understanding. • Insightful interpretations. • Logical conclusions. • Creative, conceptual observations. • Multiple points of view.	3 = balance	2 = • Some inaccuracies. • Routine observations. • Illogical or trite comments. • Confusing or unreasoned statements. • Limited, common, obvious observations. • Accepts without inquiry.	1 = incomplete

COMMENTS:

_____

_____

_____

FIGURE 6.9
AN EXAMPLE OF A SCORECARD RUBRIC
THE PROJECT CRITERIA AND SCORING GUIDE FOR THE LANE COUNTY PROJECT FAIR
(continued)

Score	C. Student demonstrates development of academic understanding and expertise.				
	5 = outstanding	4 = • Confident and knowledgeable. • Depth of understanding. • Explains in detail. • Curious, persistent. • Seeks specifics. • Pride of accomplishment.	3 = balance	2 = • Limited understanding. • Memorized responses. • Superficial treatment. • Fails to pursue answers. • Generalizes, avoids detail. • Satisfied with minimum.	1 = incomplete

COMMENTS:

_____

_____

_____

II. Learning Development and Process: How did you go about learning, and what did you use?

Score	A. Project reflects purposeful planning and effort.				
	5 = outstanding	4 = • Process appropriate to topic. • Accurate procedures. • Logical sequence of steps. • Monitors and adjusts plan. • Good time and resource management. • Focused, controlled purpose.	3 = balance	2 = • Inaccurate or inappropriate plan. • Nondeliberate trial and error. • Follows directions without understanding. • Pursues original plan regardless of results. • Lack of time and resource management. • Unsure about intent of project.	1 = incomplete

COMMENTS:

_____

_____

_____

FIGURE 6.9
AN EXAMPLE OF A SCORECARD RUBRIC
THE PROJECT CRITERIA AND SCORING GUIDE FOR THE LANE COUNTY PROJECT FAIR
(continued)

Score	B. Project documents reveal resourcefulness.				
	5 = outstanding	4 = • Variety of resources, technologies. • Develops resources. • Uses community/group resources. • Seeks out expertise, advice. • Independent learning. • Annotated listing.	3 = balance	2 = • Limited resources, nontechnical. • Lacks initiative. • Avoids input from others. • Fails to recognize or use resources. • Extensive dependence on others. • Listings without annotations.	1 = incomplete

COMMENTS:
_____
_____
_____

Score	C. Student provides evidence of problem solving and adjusting for quality.				
	5 = outstanding	4 = • Careful control/monitoring. • Self-directed thinking. • Creative problem solving. • Analytic evaluations. • Considered/tested alternatives. • Revisions improve results.	3 = balance	2 = • Haphazard management. • Dependent on directions from others. • Gives up easily or takes easiest way. • Oversimplifies or states the obvious. • Relies on best or random guesses. • Accepts errors, excuses problems.	1 = incomplete

COMMENTS:
_____
_____
_____

FIGURE 6.9
AN EXAMPLE OF A SCORECARD RUBRIC
THE PROJECT CRITERIA AND SCORING GUIDE FOR THE LANE COUNTY PROJECT FAIR
(continued)

Score	D. Student provides reflective evaluation of learning.				
	5 = outstanding	4 = • Recognizes strengths, quality of work. • Aware of weaknesses, faults. • Understands criteria, goals. • Assesses process and progress. • Sets own learning goals. • Accepts academic challenges.	3 = balance	2 = • Does not accurately identify strengths. • Minimizes weaknesses, faults. • Seems unclear about criteria, goals. • Unclear about learning process and progress. • Lets others set learning goals. • Avoids academic challenges.	1 = incomplete

COMMENTS:

_____

_____

_____

III. Presentations/Communication: In how many ways and how well can you communicate to others what you did and what you learned? (Audiovisual/computer stations will be available.)

Score	A. Written progress journal and other written products and records are effective.				
	5 = outstanding	4 = • Clear explanations. • Attention to details. • Interesting to read. • Well organized, formatted. • Helpful terminology, vocabulary. • Strong conventions.	3 = balance	2 = • Confusing explanations. • Lacking detail, clarity. • Safe, bland, trite comments. • Organizations, format weak. • Technical, unnatural, or ambiguous terms. • Language, mechanics interfere.	1 = incomplete

COMMENTS:

_____

_____

_____

FIGURE 6.9
AN EXAMPLE OF A SCORECARD RUBRIC
THE PROJECT CRITERIA AND SCORING GUIDE FOR THE LANE COUNTY PROJECT FAIR
(continued)

Score	B. Visual display and other visual compositions are effective.				
	5 = outstanding	4 = • Labels/explanations help draw attention to important points. • Display is —Balanced, colorful, attractive. —Purposefully designed. —Carefully crafted. • Artistry enhances effect.	3 = balance	2 = • Labels, explanations are lacking. • The intent is unclear and confusing. • Color, line, balance detract. • Constructed without purposeful design. • Imprecise, poor craftsmanship. • Artistic elements lacking.	1 = incomplete

COMMENTS:

_____

_____

_____

Score	C. Oral presentation and interview are effective.				
	5 = outstanding	4 = • Clear, easy to follow. • Enthusiastic, interested. • Helpful, responsive to listener. • Thoughtful, informative. • Detailed, authoritative. • Fluent, natural responses.	3 = balance	2 = • Rambling, confusing explanations. • Robotic, memorized responses. • Routine, unresponsive. • Halting, unsure. • Too superficial or too domineering. • Short, one-word responses.	1 = incomplete

COMMENTS:

_____

_____

_____

Projects may vary by age, type, and purpose.
Judges are instructed to look at *all* evidence to determine a final score.

SCORE _____
TOTAL POSSIBLE POINTS = 50

FIGURE 6.9
AN EXAMPLE OF A SCORECARD RUBRIC
THE PROJECT CRITERIA AND SCORING GUIDE FOR THE LANE COUNTY PROJECT FAIR
(continued)

PROJECT REFLECTION

<u>You may wish to make additional comments</u> about your project that will help judges understand:

- Why you chose this project.
- Any unusual or difficult things that happened during the project.
- How you feel about the results of the project.
- How others feel about your project.

The eight participating schools framed their work as follows:

1. Each school would identify one particular site for a long-term study.

2. Core team members would begin to explore one topic for in-depth study at that site (i.e., salmon migration, western pond turtles, prairie wetlands, or early human inhabitants).

3. All students at each site would begin their study with the hydrologic cycle; in particular, how water is captured, stored, and released in the Willamette Watershed.

4. Following a study of the water cycle, students would then map their site in detail and identify the specific elements of the site including soil, vegetation, wildlife, climate, and water quality.

5. The focus of the study would then shift to uses of the watershed: agriculture, forestry, recreation, and urban uses (water systems and electricity).

6. In-depth studies unique to each particular site would be completed throughout the project.

7. The studies would end by exploring natural resources management and public policy planning.

8. The results of the project would be exhibited at the Museum of Natural History as a way to showcase student studies to an authentic community audience interested in the topics. (See a graphic representation of the first three years of the project in Figure 6.10, pp. 132–133.)

"From a Drop of Rain" Emerges as the Theme of the Exhibit

In our second year, we soon discovered that constructing a culminating, interactive exhibit at the museum wouldn't happen without a lot of planning. We had to address a number of key elements unique to museum exhibitions with teachers and students. To do this, we designed a course of study for a core team of teachers and selected students, who then returned to their home schools and trained others. The course, incorporating five full days over four months, covered numerous topics that prepared them for their Info Out sharing in the exhibit.

• *Day One: What is a museum? What makes a good exhibit?* Core teams visited three local museums and identified aspects of effective museum exhibits.

• *Day Two: How do we develop a story line?* A consultant from an exhibition design company worked with the core teams in developing the story line: "From the Watersheds of the McKenzie and Willamette Rivers, a story emerges of life cycles and human impact." See Figure 6.11 (p. 134) for the story line used in the prototype development.

• *Day Three: What is the history of local native peoples?* A professor of anthropology from the University of Oregon spoke with team members about the 9,000-year history of native peoples in the Willamette Valley of Oregon. He also shared how this information has been translated into museum exhibitions.

What technologies might we use in our exhibit? Again, team members, working in three groups, rotated from station to station to learn about digital cameras and computers, mature photography basics, and use of manipulatives in museum exhibits.

• *Day Four: How might we keep accurate and informative field data to incorporate into our exhibit?* Presenters shared examples of and techniques for creating historical journals and nature field journals (See Chapter 4 for some high school biology examples). Focus topics included creative writing, nature collages, and Xerox transfer techniques.

How will our individual ideas come together in the total exhibit? Participants helped generate an overall outline of various museum modules as they related to the theme: From a Drop of Rain: A Tale of Two Rivers. See Figure 6.11 (p. 134) for an outline of the exhibit modules.

• *Day Five:* Each participating school shared its prototype module and received feedback on how to improve it. The group explored how to evaluate the quality of the prototypes and the actual museum exhibit when it was completed.

Whoa! How Might We Evaluate a Maxi-Task Like This?

Betty worked with a small group of teachers to begin exploring ways to evaluate the museum project. She shared a process for creating a scoring guide from scratch. Our goal was to create a scoring mechanism that could be used in a number of different settings. Our process had four steps.

1. Identify the Critical Traits of a Strong Performance.

First, we set about to specify the essential traits of a strong performance—in our case, of a strong museum exhibit. The program staff from the museum, Patty Krier and Cindy Gabai, were invaluable in helping us identify the following three traits of a strong museum exhibit: story line, objects, and interactives. While the end product—the exhibit modules—were important to assess, teachers were also committed to assessing the *process* that small groups of students used to develop them. (Remember the coin model used in

Chapter 1 to distinguish between content and process.) Therefore, we added the following process-oriented traits to the list: work plan and time lines, collaboration, and prototype development. We also generated a list of key questions to accompany each exhibit trait.

2. Explore Scoring Devices and Select Assessment List

Next, we examined scoring devices that could be used singly or in combination with others, and we selected an assessment list. We have described each of these devices in previous chapters. Let's review our choices in Figure 6.12 (p. 135).

We agreed to construct a checklist for students to use throughout the process based on the six traits and the key questions we had generated and then to create a weighted assessment list to score the project as a whole.

3. Construct a Draft of the Scoring Device

Our next step was to create a draft of the scoring device, including students in the process when appropriate. As part of the five-day museum class we offered, described earlier, participating staff and students visited several area museums and practiced using the above criteria in order to internalize what "good exhibits looked like." At the end of the visits, the whole group reviewed each element and commented about what made some exhibits superior to others. After the class, a small group developed the Museum Exhibit Assessment List of Traits and Key Questions shown in Figure 6.13 (pp. 136–138). We hope that educators in many different schools who use exhibits as culminating tasks will try this list. If you use it and like it, let us know.

4. Use the Scoring Device with a Project and Revise It

Finally, teachers used the scoring device with a project and are revising it as needed. We antici-pated that, in most cases, students would be more than eager to help improve it. We wanted to ask them to identify language that was ambiguous or confusing. We also wanted them to argue the merits of the weighted scoring. However, the attention that the exhibit drew from the community was so exciting for students that we were unable to get them to focus on revising the guide at the end of the school year. When the governor came to visit, the revisions were set "on the back burner."

We have shared with you how to create a performance task from scratch. We also shared with you three large-scale tasks that you may be able to use or adapt in your setting: the In-Class Homelessness Task, the Countywide Project Fair, and the Community-Based Museum Exhibit. These types of large-scale assessments require creativity, inventiveness, and energy, but they're worth it! Just think back to your own K–12 schooling experiences. We will bet that these types of projects come to mind as the most memorable and meaningful of your learning career.

Snapshot of Chapter 6

In this chapter we have

• Described performance tasks that incorporate many Info Out modes in a large-scale substantive synthesis project

• Described three types of large-scale maxi-tasks: in-class, county-wide, and community-based

• Given you a step-by-step approach for developing a good task

• Shared two new scoring devices, the Concept Acquisition Developmental Continuum (fig. 6.6) and the Scorecard Rubric (or Project Criteria and Scoring Guide [fig. 6.9])

• Shared a process for creating your own scoring devices

FIGURE 6.10
FROM A DROP OF RAIN: A TALE OF TWO RIVERS PROJECT

Scientific Investigations
• The nature of scientific investigations
• Pure scientific studies and their relationship to natural resource management
• In-depth studies
• Orientation to sites— mapping
populations counts
field journals

Writing
• Technical reports
• Poetry
• Informative interpretive guides

Problem Solving
• Identifying problems or issues
• Generating possible solutions
• Selecting appropriate solution option and developing action plan

1996–1998
A Tale of Two Rivers: The McKenzie and Willamette Watersheds

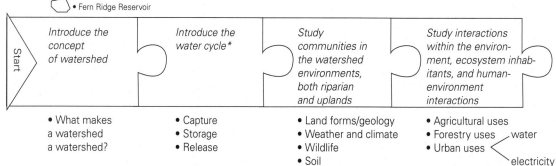

| Introduce the concept of watershed | Introduce the water cycle* | Study communities in the watershed environments, both riparian and uplands | Study interactions within the environment, ecosystem inhabitants, and human-environment interactions |

• What makes a watershed a watershed?

• Capture
• Storage
• Release

• Land forms/geology
• Weather and climate
• Wildlife
• Soil
• Plants

• Agricultural uses
• Forestry uses
• Urban uses — water, electricity

*Draw from/use/adapt the Governor's Water Enhancement Board's Watershed Curriculum.

FIGURE 6.10
FROM A DROP OF RAIN: A TALE OF TWO RIVERS PROJECT *(continued)*

Public Policy Planning
• Understanding multiple perspectives
• Analyzing issues systematically
• Understanding key concepts
• Developing an action plan

Substantive Synthesis Project
• Design an exhibit for the University of Oregon Natural History Museum
• Action project unique to site

1996–1998
A Tale of Two Rivers: The McKenzie and Willamette Watersheds *(continued)*

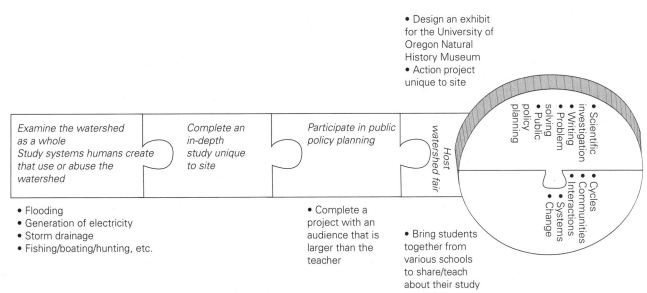

• Design an exhibit for the University of Oregon Natural History Museum
• Action project unique to site

Examine the watershed as a whole
Study systems humans create that use or abuse the watershed

Complete an in-depth study unique to site

Participate in public policy planning

Host watershed fair

• Scientific investigation
• Writing
• Problem solving
• Public policy planning

• Cycles
• Communities
• Interactions
• Systems
• Change

• Flooding
• Generation of electricity
• Storm drainage
• Fishing/boating/hunting, etc.

• Complete a project with an audience that is larger than the teacher

• Bring students together from various schools to share/teach about their study

1. What is a watershed?
2. What are the parts of a watershed, and what are their relationships to one another?
3. How do inhabitants in these communities interact with one another?
4. What characterizes human/environment interactions in the watershed?
5. In what ways can humans interact with the watershed over time to preserve it?

FIGURE 6.11
FROM A DROP OF RAIN: A TALE OF TWO RIVERS
PERFORMANCE TASK OUTLINE OF MUSEUM MODULES

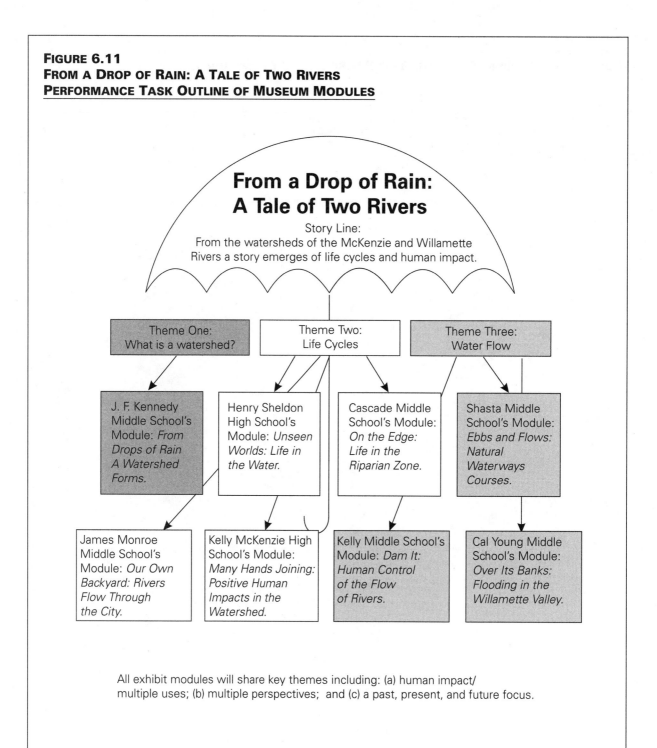

From a Drop of Rain: A Tale of Two Rivers

Story Line:
From the watersheds of the McKenzie and Willamette Rivers a story emerges of life cycles and human impact.

Theme One:
What is a watershed?

Theme Two:
Life Cycles

Theme Three:
Water Flow

J. F. Kennedy Middle School's Module: *From Drops of Rain A Watershed Forms.*

Henry Sheldon High School's Module: *Unseen Worlds: Life in the Water.*

Cascade Middle School's Module: *On the Edge: Life in the Riparian Zone.*

Shasta Middle School's Module: *Ebbs and Flows: Natural Waterways Courses.*

James Monroe Middle School's Module: *Our Own Backyard: Rivers Flow Through the City.*

Kelly McKenzie High School's Module: *Many Hands Joining: Positive Human Impacts in the Watershed.*

Kelly Middle School's Module: *Dam It: Human Control of the Flow of Rivers.*

Cal Young Middle School's Module: *Over Its Banks: Flooding in the Willamette Valley.*

All exhibit modules will share key themes including: (a) human impact/ multiple uses; (b) multiple perspectives; and (c) a past, present, and future focus.

FIGURE 6.12
CHARACTERISTICS OF SEVEN PERFORMANCE-BASED SCORING DEVICES

Analytical Trait Scoring Rubric	• This rubric includes a combination of single rubrics corresponding to each dimension, or trait, being scored. • Each trait rubric contains a scale and descriptors of each level of performance. • The scaling system contains from 3 to 6 points and assesses a range of performances from weak to strong. • This rubric can be *task-specific* (crafted for a particular project) or *generic* (designed to evaluate one type of performance, for example, writing across the curriculum).
Developmental Scoring Rubric	• This rubric is designed to be *longitudinal*—showing progress over time. • Generally a number of traits are embedded in one scale. • A large number of stages or bands assess a range of performance from "like a beginner" to "like an expert." • Younger students score on the lower bands of the scale, and older students score in the higher ranges.
Checklist	• A checklist specifies traits that must be present in a performance. • The assessor simply checks off the presence or absence of critical traits listed.
Assessment List	• An assessment list is similar to a checklist in that it indicates to students the essential traits of excellence. • A weighted scoring value is assigned for each trait.
Scorecard Rubric	• This rubric contains analytical traits and a scoring scale. • A point system provides an overall score, which can then be converted into a percentage or letter grade.
ChecBric	• A ChecBric is a combined scoring rubric and checklist. • The presence or absence of a particular trait is noted in one column. The assessment of that trait's quality is in the other column.
Holistic Scoring Rubric	• A holistic rubric includes one general descriptor for performance as a whole. • One scale is present, and one score is assigned for the entire performance.[1]

[1]We have not provided specific examples of holistic scoring rubrics in this text. We rarely use them. However, others report that they do and are pleased with the results.

John Wetten Elem.
Gladstone, OR

FIGURE 6.13
MUSEUM EXHIBIT ASSESSMENT LIST

1. Story Line	Yes	No	Points Possible	Points Earned
• Is there a clear title, and does the title make the content and focus of the exhibit clear?			3	
• Do the text and labels relate to what is seen?			3	
• Do the words encourage the visitor to view the exhibit?			3	
• Does the text provide basic information in an easy-to-read format?			3	
• Is the text in small chunks (less than 100 words) with headings, captions, and instructions?			3	
• Can the main points of the exhibit be easily identified?			3	
• Were the main ideas presented using objects, written information, and interactives?			3	
• Did the method of presenting the main ideas in this exhibit help convey the main ideas?			3	
			Total Score	

2. Interpretive Brochure	Yes	No	Points Possible	Points Earned
• Can the main points of the exhibit be easily identified in the brochure?			3	
• Is the text in small chunks (less than 100 words) with headings, captions, and instructions?			3	
• Does the text provide basic information in an easy-to-read format?			3	
• Do the graphics contribute to the overall understanding of the main ideas in the exhibit?			3	
			Total Score	

FIGURE 6.13
MUSEUM EXHIBIT ASSESSMENT LIST *(continued)*

3. Objects	Yes	No	Points Possible	Points Earned
• Do the objects help illustrate the exhibit?			3	
• Are they interesting?			3	
• Can the objects be touched? Does touching or not touching the objects affect the overall exhibit?			3	
• Are the objects displayed in such a way as to attract the visitor's attention?			3	
			Total Score	

4. Interactives	Yes	No	Points Possible	Points Earned
• Are there interactives: portions that require the visitor to do something in order to participate?			3	
• Is each interactive durable and in good working order?			3	
• Are the instructions for using the interactives clear and easy to understand?			3	
• Does the interactive directly relate to the main theme of the exhibit?			3	
			Total Score	

5. Work Plan and Time Lines

• Did your group have a work plan, and did you follow it?			6	
• Were you able to meet the time lines identified in your work plan?			6	
			Total Score	

137

FIGURE 6.13
MUSEUM EXHIBIT ASSESSMENT LIST *(continued)*

6. Collaboration	Yes	No	Points Possible	Points Earned
• Were you able to solve conflicts when they arose in your group?			6	
• Did you all share the workload, or did some members of the group do more work than others?			6	
			Total Score	

7. Prototype Development	Yes	No	Points Possible	Points Earned
• Did your group draft a number of ideas, possibilities, and sketches?			4	
• Did you keep a processfolio of your work?			4	
• Did you revise and edit your work?			4	
• Did you develop a prototype and present it to the class?			4	
			Total Score	

Overvall Score

Student Reflection:
Make additional comments here that will help the judges understand your work better.

Judges' Comments:

Take a few minutes, and jot down your reflections on this chapter. Here are some questions to consider:

1. How might I use these ideas in my setting? How could I adapt these three examples to make them more manageable for me?

2. What do I think of the Scorecard Rubric as a scoring device?

3. Might I be able to use the UmbrellaTella and Consensus Definition with my classes?

4. What am I going to take with me from this chapter on my own assessment journey?

5. What questions do I want to explore soon?

7 Sparkles and Blemishes

➤ **Implementation strengths and weaknesses**
➤ **Where to next?**

A Universal Teacher Story

A student approaches a teacher and asks a question—sometimes politely, other times more demandingly, and sometimes even suspiciously.

"What grade did you give me?"

"*Give* me ..." The words resonate menacingly. As if the teacher randomly tossed out grades to the students. As if all teachers merely fling out the grades—here are some *B's*, many *C's*, and pitifully too few *A's*.

Too many of our students do not understand the concept of connecting grades to an *earned* academic performance. They have difficulty evaluating their own performance because they are often unclear about what is being evaluated.

So they assume their teachers *give out* grades.

And, sadly, we teachers share the responsibility for this misconception. If students are not clear about the performance expectations their teachers hold for them, then they will have little chance of recognizing how well they are doing. If students do not clearly understand "what good looks like," then they won't know if they're "doing good," and will have to rely on asking, "What grade did you give me?"

To improve students' understanding of what we expect them to do, how well they should be able to do it, and how they should go about accomplishing it—is what this book on classroom-based performance assessment has been all about.

Classroom-Based Performance Assessment

As we have explained, classroom-based performance assessment is an approach to teaching and learning that stems from *our* curriculum and instruction, not from somewhere else, far away from where we teach and our students learn.

It is this connection to the classroom that makes this assessment system work:

• It informs our students exactly what we expect them to be able to do.

• It leads them to those expectations through abundant, guided practice, and reveals to them how they will be scored in advance of their performance.

• It is designed to lead to *great performances*, many of which we have proudly shared with you in the preceding chapters.

But we promised you an honest journey. Not only are there benefits, advantages, to this approach. There also are difficulties with what we have advocated—difficulties we continue to wrestle with. So let's review both the sparkles and the blemishes, the strengths and the weaknesses, of classroom-based performance assessments.

Sparkles

As you know, we have found a number of reasons for using classroom-based performance assessments.

1. The Great Motivator. First, performance tasks are a turn-on for students. Good tasks motivate kids to work hard to perform at their highest possible level. Tasks that are new, different, and even fun surprise students who think they've "done it all" in school. Engaging tasks capture their interest, their energy, and their pride of ownership. This is welcome news to classroom teachers who struggle to engage disengaged learners.

2. Accurate, Meaningful Indicators. Because performance tasks are aligned to the curriculum, they are accurate and meaningful indicators of "who knows what," and "who can do what." And when tasks are aligned to learning standards—whether the standards be national, state, or local—the performance improves. When students, their parents, and school personnel all know what the academic targets are, then everyone can get down to the business of hitting those targets. Performance tasks are the arrows that students aim and shoot at the targets.

3. Teacher Confidence in Assessment. Performance task assessment increases teacher confidence in assessing student learning. The feedback we receive from assessing our students' performance using well-constructed performance tasks is solid when those tasks meet the five criteria from Chapter 1:

Criteria 1: They offer some degree of student choice.
Criteria 2: They require both the elaboration of content knowledge and the use of processes.
Criteria 3: They reveal the explicit scoring criteria in advance.
Criteria 4: They provide an audience beyond the teacher.
Criteria 5: They are accurate indicators of targeted outcomes.

In addition to receiving feedback on student learning, we also get feedback on how well we're teaching. Performance tasks inform assessment and instruction simultaneously. This information increases our confidence in knowing how effective, or ineffective, our instruction is. And given the public's great interest in how well we are doing, this information is critical.

4. Linking Content and Process. Next, performance tasks require learners to integrate content and process. Good tasks link them together. Instead of merely regurgitating content back (like on a test or quiz), students must *apply* that newly learned content in a meaningful way by using a process, such as the writing process to write an article about the findings of a science experiment or the speaking process to create an oral presentation on a contemporary community issue.

We love how performance tasks force learners to put their knowledge to use. When kids use a process to reveal their understanding of content knowledge, they learn more deeply. Whether the process involves speaking, writing, performing, or constructing visual representations, our students learn the content better, remember it longer, and are more able to perform as adults would in the real world. It is the analysis, the synthesis, the creation, the application that moves students to deeply process the content. We must not forget that in the real world, they will be expected to *do* things—to put information to *use*—not just remember things.

5. Info In Together with Info Out. Performance tasks merge Info In and Info Out. After students learn new content information through the Info In processes (reading, listening, viewing, and manipulating), they are expected to reveal their understanding of the new knowledge in a task that applies an Info In process (writing, speaking, visual representation, or construction). This merger strengthens the link between student learning and teacher assessment of that learning.

6. Distinguishing Performance from Effort. A final sparkle relates to the burning question, "What grade did you give me?" Not only do many students fail to connect their effort to earning a grade, but they also do not distinguish effort from performance. There is a huge difference between trying hard and performing well. Good effort does not always translate into great performance. Ask any disappointed athlete, actor, or artist.

Performance task assessment separates the effort from the performance, the practice from the game, the rehearsal from show time. While it is most definitely true that good effort, as in good practice, will increase the chances of a great performance, effort and performance are two different things. And while effort is a behavior we all want to instill in our students, *performance* is critical. It is the ability to do what we expect of our students—and the ability to do it well. Through classroom-based tasks, students learn how to perform with mathematics, literature, science, and history to reveal what they know and what they can do.

Blemishes

As we have demonstrated throughout this book, not every performance turns out to be a "great" one. As much as we believe in performance assessment, we recognize that it has some weaknesses and challenges, or blemishes.

1. The Effort/Performance Gap. One sparkle leads to a blemish: distinguishing between effort and performance can cause problems. Many students, and certainly many of their parents, believe that if you try hard—that is, you do your homework, attend school regularly, and are well behaved—then you'll get a good grade. And, for the most part, they are right! We *do* tend to reward effort; if you do the work, you'll accumulate enough points, or earn a high enough percentage to earn an *A* or a *B*, or whatever high grade symbol the school uses.

But how many of us who use letter grades for reporting student achievement have felt that awkward sensation of inaccuracy as we fill out a report card with high grades for a student who, even though he or she has earned the points, when asked to perform, often fails to clear the bar? Or what about the low grade earning kid, who lacks consistent effort, misses too many assignments, and may even cause periodic disruption, but who can nail a target when the chips are down?

This is the dreaded gap between effort and performance. Our difficulty is how to bridge that gap, so that performance task assessment does not get accused of undermining education-as-we-know-it by confusing kids, their parents, and the general public.

The question is: *Can we measure actual performance while continuing to reinforce good effort, a good attitude, and good classroom behavior?*

2. The Letter Grade/Performance Score Gap. Given the difference between two assessment systems (letter grades and task scores), can and should teachers convert performance task scores into letter grades for reporting purposes?

Letter grades are summative evaluations, a more permanent label: they tell a student (and a parent) where he or she ended up in comparison to others. Performance task scores are formative—they tell the learner how well he or she did on a specific task, not compared to other students, but in relationship to a standard at a particular time.

We are in a period of transition: the old letter-grade system needs adjustment to include indicators of performance to supplement its indicators of effort. This transition will not come easily. Students (especially *A* and *B* students), their parents, and the public like report cards with letter grades. And for good reason: they understand what an *A*, *B*, *C*, and so on, means. They don't yet know, for example, about a 6-point "scoring rubric" to assess a midi-task that requires a kid to "reveal content knowledge" by actually putting it to use, say in an oral presentation. The problem we will certainly face is guiding the public through this transition without alienating people.

What about the possibility of merging the two systems in the transition? More practically, can performance task scores be weighted, so that they can be converted in numerical values or percentages for letter grades? The gurus of performance assessment strongly advise us not to because they are two different systems: do not mix apples with oranges.

Yet many classroom teachers who value performance task assessment still must fill out report cards with letter grades for each grading period. What should they do? This is a gigantic problem facing advocates of performance assessment.

The question becomes: *Can the report card be changed from letter grades to performance task scores? Or, can the report card indicate both letter grades and task scores?*

3. The Time Crunch. Because it takes time to create solid tasks with accurate scoring mechanisms and to score the tasks uniformly, how are teachers expected to do this during an already hectic school day?

With all the philosophical debate around the potential benefits of performance assessment, will its success boil down to dependency on time? Our position is that if teachers don't have adequate time to implement classroom-based performance assessment, then it won't happen.

The issue looms before us: *Will we get enough time to do it right?*

4. The Reliability Issue. If performance tasks are to gain acceptance from students, parents, the public, as well as from educators, they must be shown to be reliable indicators of student abilities. But what happens if they are not shown to be scored in a fair, accurate, and consistent manner?

To ensure reliability, teams of teachers will need time to practice scoring tasks together with accurate scoring mechanisms, so that they can calibrate their scoring, much like judges do in sports competitions. Students in Mrs. Miller's 5th grade classroom likely will earn different scores on the same assignment than Mr. Gonzales' 5th graders across the hall. The challenge for this new performance assessment system is to make it overt—that is, public, obvious, and consistently applied—to correct the subjectivity of the older assessment methods by building in objectivity through common tasks with shared rubrics.

The question becomes: *Will teachers get the training, practice, and technical support on how to score tasks objectively, fairly, consistently—that is, reliably?*

5. The Territorial Issue. Great performance tasks that can do the above will become valuable property. Just as certain paperback novels are often "claimed" by certain grade levels or certain instructional units "belong" to certain teachers, some tasks will likewise be staked out by individuals or teams. Ownership of great tasks then becomes territorial: "You can't use the comic strip task in 3rd grade because I already use it with my 4th graders."

The challenge will be to allocate effective tasks across the grades, to adapt the good ones for different subjects, and even to allow some tasks to be repeated across some grades.

The issue is: *Can we avoid turf wars as performance assessment gains popularity?*

6. Unmotivated Performers. Performance tasks are designed to highly motivate students to reveal what they know and what they can do with that knowledge, but what if the tasks do not inspire some students to reach their highest possible level?

A huge incentive for moving to performance tasks is that they are new, novel, and fun—they entice kids to want to perform well. But in reality, how can performance assessment possibly become a panacea for the segment of disinterested, under-performing, and sometimes lost children who come to our schools? Their problems vary, and the responsibility for finding solutions to those loom-ing problems remains elusive. Performance assess-ment will reach some of these kids by clearly informing them of what they are to do, how well they are expected to do it, and, most important, how to accomplish it. But it won't reach, let alone rescue, all of them.

The issue before us becomes: *Will the perform-ance task assessment system increase the performance of students who are presently underperforming suffi-ciently to earn our respect, or will it further divide our nation's children into haves and have-nots?*

7. Missed Targets. Even when students are motivated to perform well, what happens to those students who fail to hit a target, and it's time to move on to the next target?

Say the teacher has created a solid task that meets the five criteria noted earlier with a clear performance task instruction sheet, and an accu-rate scoring device, and that teacher has provided task models to evaluate, good coaching, and am-ple target practice. What should he or she do with the 2–3, 5–6, or 7–10, or more kids in her class who earn scores below the standard? And it's time to begin instruction and assessment of the next tar-geted standard?

It's like when the show is over, the troupe has packed up, and it's headed to the next town. But a significant numbers of performers didn't "get it right." What do you do with them? What reteach-ing can occur in the context of "moving on"?

Teachers have always faced this issue: what happens to students who fail the test? Do they re-ceive reteaching and retesting? Performance task

assessment promises better feedback to students, so they can improve their performance. How is this pulled off in an overcrowded classroom with an overcrowded curriculum?

The issue is: *What are we going to do with those kids who don't hit the targets?* Will teachers really be able to use task results to do a better job of re-coaching those students to lead them to higher levels of performance?

8. The Equity Issue. If students are to be held to high standards of performance, will all students be given an equal attempt at hitting the targets? And if not, is performance task assessment really an improvement over the traditional assessment measures?

Performers are supposed to be given an even playing field, so they have an equal opportunity to perform well. But, in reality, we know that this is far from true. Some kids lack good coaching; some teachers are better coaches than others at provid-ing adequate guidance on hitting the targets. Some student performers lack adequate training facili-ties. Not all schools have adequate classrooms, labs, books, and so on.[1] Some kids lack apprecia-tive and supportive fans; that is, parents and sig-nificant others who are welcome at and connected to their children's school, pro-education commu-nity organizations, and supportive businesses who volunteer in the schools or give resources without strings attached.

These conditions transcend educational issues and cross into socioeconomic issues. Who do we suppose the students are who lack an even playing field and therefore are more likely to underper-form? If the answer reflects racial, gender, or class differences, then performance task assessment is dead in the water. It cannot fix the social inequities that need fixing before kids are able to perform well in school.

---

[1]If this statement surprises anyone, see Jonathan Kozol's (1991), *Savage Inequalities,* (New York: Crown Publishers).

We would never promote any assessment system without addressing the equity issue.

The issue is: *Will advocates of performance assessment be vocal participants in the continuing struggle for educational justice?*

9. The "When-Hell-Freezes-Over" Problem. We certainly are aware that not all teachers are willing or able to make the change from traditional assessment to performance assessment. Even with all the sparkles, the blemishes prohibit some of our colleagues from taking the plunge. Perhaps they are wary of yet another educational reform, or maybe they perceive the change as an increase in teacher workload and/or accountability. These are valid concerns; we recognize their effects on potential of implementation.

The difficulty arises when a school (or district) wants to go forward with performance assessment, but a significant number of players don't want to play. What can be done?

We are not advocating forcing this assessment system on anyone. Rather, we want to move forward with those colleagues who are ready and willing. But, realistically, can a school move forward with only some teachers implementing performance assessment?

The question is: *What do we do if an entire staff is not able to commit to performance assessment?*

Next Steps

Given the sparkles and blemishes of classroom-based performance assessment, where will go from here? Obviously, we will work with the sparkles of the system to make them brighter. And we are committed to work on the blemishes to heal them.

For example, the daunting issue that faces teachers who use a letter grade report card—that of converting performance task scores into letter grades—may be resolved by using weighted values for each trait on a scoring rubric. High school math teacher Pat Tuel liked our ChecBric scoring device, so she adapted it (fig. 7.1).

The weighted values allow her to convert a point score into a letter grade because her school operates with a letter grade system. Note the grading scale at the bottom of Figure 7.1.

Teachers needing the percentage/letter grade translation may select one formula that most closely matches their grading system. See Figure 7.2 for other possible formulas. This weighted ChecBric idea should be pursued—it may heal a blemish.

Another big issue—finding the time required to create, revise, and score tasks—may be improved by creating, at the district or state level, generic tasks that require the use of given processes but are open to varying content. That way, instead of creating an assessment task, a teacher could insert specific content into a predesigned one.

For example, in our district a team of teachers is creating a set of performance tasks. One literature performance task, A Novel Approach, requires students to perform a set of four mini-tasks ("Who's on First, Second, Third, Home Plate?") for note taking while reading whichever novel their teacher assigns. The maxi-task to culminate the unit is the creation of a book project, either in the written, oral, or visual Info In mode. The processes are embedded into the task, but the content is adaptable. Teachers of different grade levels with different literature content can plug in their favorite literature selections into a pre-made, ready-to-go performance task. This ready-for-teacher-adaptation task may address the "when-hell-freezes-over" problem—thawing out our more resistant colleagues.

For ease in sharing, these generic tasks can then be set out on the World Wide Web. (See District 4J's assessment site at http://www.4j.lane.edu/instruction/cando. Pilot-testing of these tasks by interested teachers will reveal whether the tasks work or need refinement. And we all get better at developing tasks when we see excellent

145

FIGURE 7.1
WEIGHTED CHECBRIC

To receive the highest score in each of the four areas, you will want to find evidence of each of these parts of a successful solution.

Conceptual Understanding ___ I used the important information to solve the task, changing it to mathematical ideas. ___ My work and solution fit what was requested in the task/question.	**Conceptual Understanding** **6**. **5**. Math concepts thoroughly developed. All relevant information used. **4**. Math concepts adequately developed. Relevant information used. **3**. Some understanding of concepts displayed. Fragments of information used. **2**. Part of task translated into inappropriate concepts. Assumptions about information may be flawed. **1**. Task translated into inappropriate concepts. Inappropriate information used. **0**. No evidence provided.
Processes and Strategies ___ I used diagrams, pictures, models and/or symbols to solve the task. ___ I used problem-solving skills/strategies that showed good reasoning.	**Processes and Strategies** **6**. **5**. Pictures, models, diagrams, or symbols clearly used to solve the task. Thoroughly developed strategies are completed. **4**. Pictures, models, diagrams, or symbols used to solve the task. Reasonable strategies are completed. **3**. Pictures, models, diagrams, or symbols partially used. Reasonable strategies partially completed. **2**. Pictures, models, diagrams, or symbols partially detract from solving the task. Strategies are ineffective. **1**. Pictures, models, diagrams, or symbols conflict with the solution. **0**. Strategies not recorded.
Communication ___ I explained what I was thinking while working on the task, including using pictures, charts, or diagrams to help explain the "why" of my steps. ___ In my solution one step seems to flow to the next.	**Communication** **6**. **5**. Reasoning behind process clearly displayed and enhanced by graphics or examples. Logical coherent presentation. **4**. Reasoning behind process is clear throughout. Clear, organized presentation. **3**. Reasoning behind process partially displayed with gaps that have to be inferred. Presentation does not follow a clear pattern or sequence. **2**. Communication focuses on the solution and does not indicate a path to the solution. **1**. The reasoning detracts from the work and may include irrelevant ideas. **0**. Reasoning not complete or provided.

FIGURE 7.1
WEIGHTED CHECBRIC *(continued)*

To receive the highest score in each of the four areas, you will want to find evidence of each of these parts of a successful solution.

Verification	Verification
___ I showed that I reviewed my solution process (and checked my calculations) to verify that my work made sense. ___ If possible, I worked the problem a different way.	**6**. **5**. Uses a different perspective to verify or support the reasonableness of the first approach. **4**. Review of work supports the original approach. No new perspective. **3**. Review of work supports the original approach; an error not detected or corrected. **2**. Checking focuses on the solution and/or check may conflict with original approach. **1**. Check of work ineffective (i.e., misses the errors). **0**. No evidence provided.

Grading scale: 6=102%, 5=90%, 4=78%, 3=66%, 2=54%, 1=45%, 0 = 30%
Formula: Percent = 12x + 30
x = average of numerical scores

models that others have developed.

To address the big issue of learning how to create accurate scoring rubrics for performance tasks, some districts and states have done the work for the classroom teacher. With the scoring rubric ready in advance, the teacher creates a task that requires the students to meet the traits stated on the rubric. For example, the Historical Persuasive Letter Task in Chapter 4 uses the Oregon Analytical Trait Scoring Guide. The How to Catch a Cold and the Civil War Newspaper Tasks both used an adapted version of the same scoring guide.

Finally, we are looking for input from you. Send us your ideas for improving classroom-based performance assessment. What suggestions do you have for addressing the blemishes?

Our Last (Happy) Story

This story was told by a teacher in a workshop we gave on classroom-based performance task assessment in her district. During a break she came up and thanked us for sharing our ideas. She went on:

"I really like to use performance tasks in my classroom to measure student understanding, and the kids are really catching on."

She continued, "Last month when I was assigning them a paper to compare two different novels they had read, one student raised her hand, and asked,

'Where's the rubric?'

I answered, 'Uh, it's not yet finished. . . . but I'm working on it, I'm working on it.' I couldn't tell them it was due to bus duty that week . . .

Another kid persisted, 'But don't you think we *need* one?'

FIGURE 7.2
SAMPLE GRADING SCALES WITH FORMULAS

6	100%	formula:	$y = 10x + 40$
5	90%		y = percent
4	80%		x = trait's score (6, 5, 4, 3, 2, or 1)
3	70%		
2	60%		
1	50%		

6	107%	formula:	$y = 12x + 35$
5	95%		y = percent
4	83%		x = trait's score (6, 5, 4, 3, 2, or 1)
3	71%		
2	59%		
1	47%		

6	101%	formula:	$y = 11x + 35$
5	90%		y = percent
4	79%		x = trait's score (6, 5, 4, 3, 2, or 1)
3	68%		
2	57%		
1	46%		

'Yeah,' more students chimed in.

So I was forced to create a rubric, with their help, on the spot.

It took a few minutes, but once we had agreement on "what good looks like," the first kid, now satisfied, said,

'Good, it wouldn't be *fair* without one.' "

When students get to this level of understanding what the expectations are—of what their targets are—they are ready to produce *great performances.*

And your students will be, too.

Snapshot of Chapter 7

In this chapter we have reviewed the sparkles (strengths) and blemishes (weaknesses) of a classroom-based performance assessment system.

• The sparkles include increased student motivation, clear alignment to the actual curriculum, increased teacher confidence in assessment, content-process linkage, Info In and Info Out linkage, and distinguishing effort from performance.

• The blemishes include student confusion over grades and performance, the time factor for busy teachers, the reliability issue, the territorial issue, unmotivated students, how to deal with students who miss the targets, the resource equity issue, and how to move forward even though some colleagues choose not to.

We also identified some next steps to consider, including the weighted ChecBric to link performance on a task to a letter grade, employing generic tasks and accompanying rubrics created at the district or state level.

Please record your thoughts about these issues.

Appendix

Oregon Writing Scoring Guide: Middle School Student Version

ORGANIZATION

Structuring information in logical sequence, making connections and transitions among ideas, sentences and paragraphs

6	5	4
The organization makes the central idea(s) and supporting details clear. The order and structure ar strong and move the reader easily through the writing. The writing has • effective (and sometimes creative) ideas, details, and examples in an order that is easy to follow. • a strong and inviting introduction that draws the reader in and a strong conclusion that leaves the reader satisfied. • smooth, effective transitions that together ideas, sentences, and paragraphs; the reader can move easily from one part to the next. • details placed where they work well and make the most sense.	The organization helps clarify the central idea(s) and supporting details. The order and structure are strong and move the reader through the writing. The writing has • ideas, details, and examples in an order that makes sense and is easy to follow. • an inviting introduction that draws the reader in and a conclusion that leaves the reader satisfied. • smooth transitions that tie together ideas, sentences, and paragraphs; the reader can move easily from one part to the next. • details placed where they work well and make the most sense.	The organization is clear and functional. Order and structure are present, but may seem like a formula. The writing has • clear sequencing. • an organization that may be predictable. • an introduction that is recognizable but may not be especially inviting; a developed conclusion that is functional but may seem repetitive and ordinary. • transitions that work but they may be awkward or common. • a body that is easy to follow with details that fit where placed. • an organization that helps the reader, despite some weaknesses.

150

ORGANIZATION (continued)

3	2	1
An attempt to organize the writing has been made, but it doesn't work well in places or is too obvious. The writing has • attempts to put ideas in order, but the order is sometimes unclear • a beginning and an ending, but they are either too short or twoo obvious (e.g., "My topic is ..."; "These are all the reasons that ...") • a limited number of transitional words that arc used too many times (e.g., "and," "then," "but," "so," "or," "for," "yet," numbering • a structure that is too obvious, almost like a formula. • details that seem out of order and confuse the reader. • an organization that helps the reader in some places but breaks down in others.	**The writing lacks a clear organizational structure. An occasional attempt at organizing is made, but the writing is difficult to follow and the reader has to reread large sections. The writing may seem incomplete. The writing has** • some attempts to organize ideas, but the order does not make the meaning clear. • a missing or extremely undeveloped introduction, body, or conclusion. • few or no transition; when present they are ineffective or overused. • details are randomly placed; the reader is frequently confused	**The writing doesn't hold together; the writing seems haphazard and disjointed. Even after rereading, the reader is still confused. The writing has** • ideas that are not in a clear or logical order. • no recognizable beginning or ending. • few or no transitions. • arrangement and pace of ideas that either drag or feel rushed.

Source: Office of Assessment and Evaluation • Oregon Department of Education • July 8, 1996

VOICE
Expressing ideas in an engaging and credible way for audience and purpose

6

The writer has chosen an appropriate voice for the topic, purpose, and audience and shows a deep sense of involvement with the topic. The writing is interesting and sincere. The writing has
- an effective level of closeness to the audience or distance from it (e.g., a narrative should have a strong personal voice, while a research paper may require a more objective voice; both should be lively or interesting).
- an exceptionally strong sense of purpose and audience.
- a sense that the topic has come to life; when appropriate, shows originality, liveliness, honesty, conviction, excitement, humor, suspense, and/or use of outside resources.

5

The writer has chosen an appropriate voice for the topic, purpose, and audience and shows involvement with the topic. The writing is interesting and seems sincere. The writing has
- an appropriate level of closeness to the audience or distance from it (e.g., a narrative should have a strong personal voice, while a researched report may require a more objective voice; both could be lively or interesting.).
- a strong sense of purpose and audience.
- a sense that the topic has come to life; when appropriate, the writing shows originality, liveliness, honesty, conviction, excitement, humor, suspense, and/or use of outside resources.

4

A voice is present, and there is a sense of involvement with the topic. In places, the writing is interesting and seems sincere. The writing has
- a questionable or inconsistent level of closeness or distance from the audience.
- a sense of purpose and audience but may not use a consistently appropriate voice.
- originality, liveliness, humor, and/or use of outside resources, when appropriate; however, at times voice may be too casual or formal.

3

The writer doesn't seem particularly involved with the topic or may seem either too personal or too impersonal. The writing has
- a voice that doesn't seem to match the topic, purpose, and audience.
- a limited sense that the paper was written for a particular audience.
- a sense in places of the writer behind the words; however, this may shift or disappear a line or two later.
- limited ability to shift from a casual, informal voice to one that is more objective when that is necessary.

2

The writing provides little sense of involvement or evidence of a suitable voice. The writing has
- little or no sense that the writer cares about the topic; the writing is largely flat, lifeless, stiff, or mechanical.
- little or no awareness of matching the topic, purpose, and audience.
- little or no sense of the writer behind the words; there are only a few places where the reader and writer can feel a connection.
- a voice that is likely to be overly formal or overly personal.

1

The writing lacks a sense of involvement and a suitable voice. The writing has
- no sense that the writer cares about the topic; the writing is flat, lifeless, stiff, or mechanical.
- no sense that the piece was written for an audience.
- no hint of the writer behind the words; there are few if any places where the reader feels connected to the writer. The writing doesn't get the reader involved.

Source: Office of Assessment and Evaluation • Oregon Department of Education • July 8, 1996

WORD CHOICE

Selecting functional, precise, and descriptive words appropriate for audience and purpose

6
Words communicate the intended message in an exceptionally interesting, accurate, and natural way. The writer uses a rich, broad range of words that have been carefully chosen and thoughtfully placed. The writing has

- accurate, powerful, and specific words; word choices make the writing interesting and lively.
- fresh, original expression; if slang is used, it is for a reason and works very well.
- vocabulary that has variety and gets noticed but is also natural and doesn't seem to be trying to impress the reader.
- ordinary words used in an unusual way.
- words that create strong pictures in the reader's mind; metaphors and similes may be used.

5
Words communicate the intended message in an interesting, accurate, and natural way. The writer uses a broad range of words that have been carefully chosen and thoughtfully placed. The writing has

- accurate, specific words; word choices make the writing more interesting and lively.
- fresh, clear expression; if slang is used, it is for a reason and works well.
- vocabulary that may have variety and get noticed but is also natural and doesn't seem to be trying to impress the reader.
- ordinary words used in an unusual way.
- words that create clear pictures in the reader's mind; metaphors and similes may be used.

4
Words communicate the intended message. The writer uses a variety of words that work and are appropriate for the topic, audience, and purpose. The writing has

- words that work but do not necessarily make the writing more interesting and lively.
- expression that works; however, slang, if used, does not always seem to match the purpose or seem effective.
- some attempts at colorful language; however, they may occasionally seem overdone.
- rare experiments with language; however, the writing may have some especially good moments, and it generally avoids clichés.

3
Language is ordinary. The writer does not use a variety of words, producing a sort of "generic" paper with commonly used words and phrases. Words may be too technical or loaded with jargon. The writing has

- words that work, but that are rarely interesting.
- expression that seems ordinary and general; any slang is used for a reason and is effective.
- words that are accurate for the most part, although misused words may sometimes appear.
- attempts at colorful language that do not fit or seem natural; they seem forced or trying to impress.
- too many clichés and overused expressions.
- overuse or ineffective use of technical jargon.

2
The language is monotonous and/or misused, taking away from the meaning and impact. The writing has

- words that are flat or not specific enough.
- words or expressions that are either so common or used so often that they detract from the message.
- images that don't work because they are not clear or are absent altogether.

1
The writing shows a limited vocabulary, or is so filled with words not used correctly that the meaning is unclear. Only the most general idea comes through because the language is not specific enough. The writing has

- general, vague words that do not make the point.
- a small set of words used over and over.
- words that simply do not work; they seem too general or just plain wrong.

Source: Office of Assessment and Evaluation • Oregon Department of Education • July 8, 1996

SENTENCE FLUENCY
Developing flow and rhythm of sentences

6

The writing has an effective flow that is smooth and natural. The sentences are put together so they are consistently varied and interesting. The sentences make the piece easy and interesting to read. The writing has
- a natural, fluent sound; it glides along with one sentence flowing effortlessly into the next.
- extensive variation in sentence lengths, patterns, and beginnings that make the writing interesting.
- a sentence structure that helps the reader understand the text by highlighting key ideas and relationships.
- strong control over sentence structure; if fragments are used at all, they work well.

5

The writing has a smooth, natural flow. Sentences are put together so they are varied and interesting. The sentences make the piece easy and interesting to read aloud. The writing has
- a natural, fluent sound; it glides along with one sentence flowing into the next.
- a variety of sentence lengths, patterns, and beginnings that make the writing interesting.
- sentence structure that helps the reader understand the meaning.
- control over sentence structure; if fragments are used at all, they work well.
- a natural-sounding dialogue, if dialogue is used at all.

4

The writing flows; however, connections between phrases or sentences may be less than fluid. Sentences are somewhat varied, making oral reading easy. The writing has
- a natural sound; the reader can move easily through the piece, although it may lack a sense of rhythm.
- some repeated sentence lengths, patterns, and beginnings that detract somewhat from overall impact.
- strong control over simple sentences; less control over more complex sentences. If fragments are used at all, they are usually effective.
- dialogue, if used at all, that usually sounds natural but can sound artificial.

3

The writing tends to be choppy rather than smooth. Sometimes awkward constructions force the reader to slow down or reread. The writing has
- some passages that are easy to read aloud and some that are choppy.
- some variety in sentence lengths, patterns, and beginnings, although a few are used repeatedly.
- simple sentence used correctly, but more complex sentences may have problems; if fragments are used, they may not be effective.
- sentences that are correct, but are not very interesting or appealing.
- dialogue that may sound unnatural or not true-to-life, if it is used.

2

The writing tends to be choppy or rambling. Awkward construction often forces the reader to slow down and reread. The writing has
- large portions of the text that are difficult to follow or read aloud.
- sentence patterns that are monotonous (e.g., subject-verb or subject-verb-object).
- a large number of awkward, choppy, or rambling sentence structures.

1

The writing is difficult to follow or to read aloud. Sentences tend to be choppy, incomplete, rambling, or just very awkward. The writing has
- sentences that may be hard to read aloud easily.
- confusing word order that often makes the meaning hard to follow.
- sentence patterns that frequently make meaning unclear.
- sentences that are fragmented, confusing, choppy, or rambling on and on.

Source: Office of Assessment and Evaluation • Oregon Department of Education • July 8, 1996

CONVENTIONS

Demonstrating knowledge of spelling, grammar, puncutation, capitalization, usage, paragraphing

6
The writing demonstrates mastery of a variety of standard conventions, even in complex and less common situations. Errors, if any, are not obvious or significant. The writing has
- correct use of punctuation, including commas, semicolons, apostrophes, and colons, in a variety of situation to add meaning.
- correct spelling, even of difficult words.
- paragraphing that strengths the impact and organization.
- correct capitalization.
- correct grammar and usage that contribute to clarity and style.
- skill in using a wide range of conventions in a sufficiently long and complex piece.
- little or no need for editing.

5
The writing demonstrates strong control of standard conventions which effectively contribute to the message. Errors are so few and so minor that they do not distract the reader. The writing has
- correct grammar and usage.
- sound paragraphing.
- effective use of punctuation.
- correct spelling, even of difficult words.
- few capitalization errors.
- skill in using a wide range of conventions in a sufficiently long and complex piece.
- little or no need for editing.

4
The writing demonstrates competent handling of standard conventions. Minor errors are distracting but not confusing. The writing has
- correct end-of-sentence punctuation; minor and very few or no instances of confusion with commas, semicolons, apostrophes, or colons.
- common or key words spelled correctly.
- paragraph breaks that are logically placed.
- correct capitalization; errors, if any, are in uncommon cases.
- occasionally incorrect grammar and usage; problems do not confuse or change the meaning.

3
The writing shows a limited control of standard conventions. Errors begin to interfere with readability. The writing has
- errors in grammar, usage, and capitalization that do not block meaning but do distract the reader.
- paragraphs that sometimes run together or begin at ineffective points.
- end-of-sentence punctuation that is usually correct, but internal punctuation contains frequent errors.
- spelling errors that distract the reader; misspelling of common words sometimes occurs.
- some control over basic conventions, but the text is too simple or too short to show mastery.
- a significant need for editing.

2
The writing shows little understanding of standard conventions. Errors often distract and confuse the reader, requiring the reader to reread passages. The writing has
- many places where punctuation is left out or incorrect.
- frequent spelling errors, even of common words.
- random paragraph indentations or none at all.
- many capitalization errors, including sentence beginnings and names.
- errors in grammar and usage that confuse the reader or change the meaning and purpose.
- a need for major revisions and corrections.

1
Numerous errors in conventions repeatedly distract the reader and make the writing difficult to read. The writing has
- very limited skill in using conventions.
- punctuation (including ends of sentences) that tends to be omitted, haphazard, or incorrect.
- frequent spelling errors that significantly interfere with readability.
- paragraphing that may be irregular or absent.
- capitalization that appears to be random.
- a need for extensive editing.

Source: Office of Assessment and Evaluation • Oregon Department of Education • July 8, 1996

CITING SOURCES

Indicating the sources of information presented, including all ideas, statements, quotes, and statistics that are taken from sources and that are not common knowledge

6

The writing demonstrates exceptionally strong commitment to the quality and significance of research and the accuracy of the written document. Documentation is used to avoid plagiarism and to enable the reader to judge how believable or important a piece of information is by checking the source. The writer has

• acknowledged borrowed material by introducing the quotation or paraphrase with the name of the authority.
• punctuated all quoted materials; errors, if any, are minor.
• paraphrased material by rewriting it using writer's style and language.
• provided specific in-text documentation for each borrowed item.
• provided a bibliography page listing every source cited in the paper; omitted sources that were consulted but not used.

5

The writing demonstrates a strong commitment to the quality and significance of research and the accuracy of the written document. Documentation is used to avoid plagiarism and to enable the reader to judge how believable or important a piece of information is by checking the source. Errors are so few and so minor that the reader can easily skim right over them unless specifically searching for them. The writer has

• acknowledged borrowed material by introducing the quotation or paraphrase with the name of the authority; key phrases are directly quoted so as to give full credit where credit is due.
• punctuated all quoted materials; errors are minor.
• paraphrased material by rewriting using writer's style and language.
• provided specific in-text documentation for borrowed material.
• provided a bibliography page listing every source cited in the paper; omitted sources that were consulted but not used.

4

The writing demonstrates a commitment to the quality and significance of research and the accuracy of the written document. Documentation is used to avoid plagiarism and to enable the reader to judge how believable or important a piece of information is by checking the source. Minor errors, while perhaps noticeable, do not blatantly violate the rules of documentation. The writer has

• acknowledged borrow material by sometimes introducing the quotation or paraphrase with the name of the authority.
• punctuated all quoted materials; errors, while noticeable, do not impede understanding.
• paraphrased material by rewriting using writer's style and language.
• provided in-text documentation for most borrowed material.
• provided in-text documentation for most borrowed material.
• provide a bibliography page listing every source cited in the paper; included sources that were consulted but not used.

3

The writing demonstrates a limited commitment to the quality and significance of research and the accuracy of the written document. Documentation is sometimes used to avoid plagiarism and to enable the reader to judge how believable or important a piece of information is by checking the source. Errors begin to violate the rules of documentation. The writer has

• enclosed quoted materials within quotation marks; however, incorrectly used commas, colons, semicolons, question marks, or exclamation marks that are part of the quoted material.
• included paraphrased material that is not properly documented.
• paraphrased material by simply rearranging sentence patterns.

2

The writing demonstrates little commitment to the quality and significance of research and the accuracy of the written document. Frequent errors in documentation result in instances of plagiarism and often do not enable the reader to check the source. The writer has

• enclosed quoted materials within quotation marks; however, incorrectly used commas, colons, semicolons, question marks, or exclamation marks that are part of the quoted material.
• attempted paraphrasing but included words that should be enclosed by quotation marks or rephrased in the writer's language and style.
• altered the essential ideas of the source.
• included citations that incorrectly identify reference sources.

1

The writing demonstrates disregard for the conventions of research writing. Lack of proper documentation results in plagiarism and does not enable the reader to check the source. The writer has

• borrowed abundantly from an original source, even to the point of retaining the essential wording.
• no citations that credit source material.
• included words or ideas from a source without providing quotation marks.
• included no bibliography page listing sources that were used.

References

Beatty, P. (1981). *Lupita Mañana*. New York: Beach Tree Books.

Bloom, B. (Ed.). (1956). *Taxonomy of educational objectives*. New York: David McKay Company, Inc.

Christensen, L. Unlearning the myths that bind us. (1991 May/June). *Rethinking Schools* 1.

Christmas day, 1492. (1984). In *A proud nation* (p. 38). Evanston, IL: McDougal, Littel, and Company.

Conrad, P. (1991). *Pedro's journal*. New York: Scholastic Books.

Dorris, M.(1992). *Morning girl*. New York: Hyperion Books for Children.

Educators in Connecticut's Pomperaug Regional School District 15. (1996). *A teacher's guide to performance-based learning and assessment* (pp. 120, 137). Alexandria, VA: ASCD.

Eugene Public School District 4J. (1995). *Education 2000 K-5 integrated curriculum*. Eugene, OR: Eugene Public School District 4J.

Fritz, J. (1983). *The double life of Pocahontas*. New York: Putnam.

Granowsky, A. (Ed.). (1993). *Point of view stories*. Austin, TX: Steck Vaughn.

Inspiration Software. Inc. *Inspiration*. Inspiration Software. 7412 S.W. Beaverton Hillsdale Hwy., Suite 102, Portland, OR 97225, 800-877-4292, http://www.inspiration.com

Marzano, R. (1994). *The systematic identification and articulation of content standards and benchmarks*. Aurora, CO: Mid-continent Regional Educational Laboratory.

Marzano, R.J., Brandt, R.S., Hughes, C.S., Jones, B.F., Presseisen, B.Z., Rankin, S.C., & Suhor, C. (1988). *Dimensions of thinking: a framework for curriculum and instruction*. Alexandria, VA: ASCD.

Marzano, R.J., Pickering, D., & McTighe, J. (1993). *Assessing student outcomes: Performance assessment using the Dimensions of Learning model*. Alexandria, VA: ASCD.

Newmann, Fred M. (1991). Linking restructuring to authentic student achievement. *Phi Delta Kappan, 72*(6), 458–463.

Ogle, D. (1986). A teaching model that develops active reading of expository text. *The Reading Teacher* (39), 564.

Oregon Department of Education, Office of Assessment and Evaluation. (1996). Writing scoring guide: Middle school student version. Salem, OR: Oregon Department of Education. (Note: Over the years the Beaverton, Oregon, School District and the Northwest Regional Educational Laboratory worked to refine and improve Oregon's Analytical Trait Writing Scoring Guide.)

Oregon Department of Education (1997a). *Common curriculum goals and content standards*. Salem, OR: Oregon Department of Education (255 Capitol St., N.E., Salem, OR 97310-0203, 503-378-3310).

Oregon Department of Education (1997b). *Teacher support for Oregon standards newspaper.* Salem, OR: Author.

Oregon Department of Education (1998, September). *Oregon state standards.* Salem, OR: Author.

Scieszka, J. (1989). *The true story of the three little pigs.* New York: Viking.

Shoemaker, B.J., and Lewin, L. (1993). Curriculum and assessment: two sides of the same coin. *Educational Leadership, 50*(8), 55–57.

Snyder, T. *Timeliner.* Tom Snyder Productions, 80 Coolidge Hill Rd., Watertown, MA 12172, 800-342-0236

Stiggins, R. J. (1994). *Student-centered classroom assessment.* New York: Merrill.

Sunburst Communication, Inc. *Expression.* Sunburst Communication, Inc. 101 Castleton St., P.O. Box 100, Pleasantville, NY 10570, 1-800-321-7511, http://sunburstonline.com

White, E. B. (1952). *Charlotte's web.* New York: Harper and Row.

Wiggins, G. (September 1995). Shared at a CLASS Workshop, San Antonio, Texas. The Center on Learning, Assessment, and School Structure, 648 The Great Rd., Princeton, NJ 08540.

Index

Page numbers in boldface refer to pages that include figures.

About the Authors

Larry Lewin, a classroom teacher of 24 years, teaches integrated language arts/history and computer classes at Monroe Middle School in Eugene, Oregon. He also is a staff development trainer who conducts seminars and workshops nationally. Larry has consulted with hundreds of schools in more than 35 states on such timely topics as performance assessment, teaching with computer technology, integrated thematic curriculum, and a strategic approach to the reading/writing process. He is the co-author of three textbooks on the writing process for the Stack the Deck Writing Program, and he has published articles in *Educational Leadership, The Reading Teacher, Language Arts,* and other journals. He may be contacted at 2145 Lincoln St., Eugene, OR 97405. Phone: 541-343-1577. E-mail: llewin@teleport.com

Betty Jean Shoemaker has taught in special education, elementary, and middle level classrooms since 1965. Dr. Shoemaker is currently a Curriculum Coordinator for Eugene, Oregon, School District 4J. In this capacity she provides instructional leadership districtwide. She works with teachers K-12 in curriculum development and staff development. Betty facilitated the development of the district's elementary integrated curriculum framework, the *Education 2000, K-5 Integrated Curriculum,* the district's *Middle School 2000 Curriculum Framework,* and is currently working with teachers to develop computer-based developmental report cards and performance assessment composite records. She earned her Ph.D. at the University of Oregon in Curriculum and Instruction. She consults nationally in the areas of integrated thematic curriculum and performance-based assessment. She has published work in *Phi Delta Kappan, Educational Leadership,* and *Roeper Review,* as well as monographs and edited collections. She may be contacted at Eugene Public Schools, 200 N. Monroe St., Eugene, OR 97402-4295. Phone: 541-687-3455. Fax: 541-338-9749. E-mail: Shoemaker@4J.lane.edu